Developing Vocational Instruction

Robert F. Mager

Kenneth M. Beach, Jr.

 Lear Siegler, Inc./Fearon Publishers

Belmont, California

ISBN-0-8224-2060-0

Library of Congress Catalog Card Number: 67-26846

Printed in the United States of America.

Foreword

Within the pages of this book will be found what is, perhaps, the very first attempt to make available to the vocational educator the essence of modern educational technology ... in language that he can understand. Much has happened during the past fifteen years or so to cause instruction to move from an art toward a technology. Where guesswork was the order of the day, there are now systematic bases on which to make decisions about what a course should contain in the way of content, depth of treatment, selection of procedures, student evaluation, and course improvement.

Developing Vocational Instruction doesn't say it all. To do so would require book-length treatment of each of the steps described. But the authors have done an excellent job of describing succinctly each of the steps involved in the systematic development of instruction. They have provided examples from a variety of fields, and have included references that will help the reader expand his competence. Perhaps most significantly, the material is presented in plain English. This is no small favor in an age where pedantic ponderosity seems to be the order of the day, where the burden of understanding so often is placed squarely on the reader. It is no trick or accomplishment to say things that no one will understand. It *is* something of an accomplishment to be able to say things in a way most people will understand, and that is what I believe the authors have done in this book.

The steps of the instructional process described in these pages are those used by some of the best-known training consulting firms, by trainers in industry, and by some sections of the military. The procedure is as applicable to academic as to vocational areas, and its use is certain to lead to course improvements.

Vocational and technical educators are in a position to become leaders among professional instructors. That they should act to do so is timely . . . the tools are at hand. This is one of them.

JAMES D. FINN, Chairman
Vocational Education Committee
Educational Media Council

Preface

When we consider the qualities that make a successful teacher, the issue is fraught with difficulty. Qualities such as sincerity, efficiency, courage, resolution, energy, tact, and personality all spring to mind. The list is seemingly endless, and even after having compiled it no one really is sure of how it can be used.

A more useful approach is to consider what a teacher actually *does*; in other words, to adopt a "functions" rather than a "qualities" approach, and then to make sure that these functions are carried out in the most efficient, effective, and economical manner possible.

Basically there are but two kinds of activity in which a teacher can engage; teachers either *manage* learning resources, or else they *operate* as a resource. Bertrand Russell put this neatly when he said:

Work is of two kinds: first, altering the position of matter at or near the earth's surface relative to other such matter; second, telling other people to do so. The first kind is unpleasant and ill paid; the second is pleasant and highly paid.

The moral should not be lost on teachers!

When a teacher deliberately creates a learning environment in his classroom with a view to realizing predefined objectives, he is acting as a manager. When the same person physically teaches in that classroom, he then becomes one of his own resources and takes on the role of an operator. He is saying, in effect, that he is the most appropriate resource available, more appropriate at realizing the objectives than any textbook, workbook, program, film, tape, or record obtainable. On some occasions this will probably be true, but too often a teacher decides to engage in "talk and chalk" because he enjoys talking: the decision to be a teacher-operator is taken on the basis of personal preference rather than on the needs of the learning situation. The danger lies not so much in the fact that teachers operate; we all have to do this at times. The danger lies in the fact that they may do more operating work than they should or the situation calls for.

Since the time available and the capacities of teachers must always be limited, it follows that they should concentrate, as far as possible, upon doing that work which stems from their unique organizational role as managers of resources for learning. Viewed in this way, it is possible to isolate and identify the four functions of the teacher-manager:

Planning
Organizing
Leading
Controlling

When the teacher-manager "plans," he attempts to forecast future requirements, define the objectives which will have to be realized, write a syllabus of instruction, determine the order in which topics will be studied, allocate the time available, and budget for the resources involved. Organizing is a far simpler activity. It involves the deliberate creation of a learning environment, and delegation of responsibilities. At the same time, the most effective relationships must be established among the people involved in the educational system.

Probably the most skilled work that the teacher-manager performs, and certainly the most personal, lies in the guidance, encouragement, and inspiration which he communicates to his students. In this way, the teacher makes decisions as to how the objectives can best be accomplished, communicates them to his students, and then motivates them sufficiently so as to get them to accept responsibility for their own learning. This leadership function is important; well-led students do learn without plans and organization, but well-led pupils backed by good plans and organization become outstanding. The controlling function is concerned with the need to check performance against previously established criteria, with a view to determining whether or not the objectives have been realized.

The four functions of the teacher-manager are separate and disparate activities, but together they make up the whole of the educational management process. Such a philosophy introduces the concept of management by results into education, and allows for the formulation of a single theory of instruction capable of providing what the Senate Subcommittee on Economic Progress described as

... guiding principles for development and application of educational technology, (which) would contribute immeasurably to healthy development of new systems and would help avoid waste of resources.

Now that the functions of the teacher-manager have been considered, it is possible to consider how the resources that are available to him can be most effectively utilized. For a very long time, most efforts were concerned with polished and elegant attempts to mechanize the process of teaching through the production of teaching and learning aids. Such devices, however, ought to be considered less as aids and more as part of the new technology promising to transform the present day concepts and methods employed by the teacher.

All too often we have been accustomed to think of things as existing apart from what they actually do or accomplish. We tend to think of the chalkboard, the language laboratory, and the teaching machine as something quite apart from each other and from the system of which they are part. A more meaningful approach is to take a whole view of the learning system and then to determine how each of the constituent parts interacts. Isolated parts can rarely provide adequate information about the system, but the system can certainly provide extremely valuable information about the functions which can or must be fulfilled by each component. Just as an atom can only be described in terms of activity, so can the resources of an educational environment be more fruitfully described in terms of what they do and the role they fulfill in realizing the system's objectives.

Criticisms of these resources have normally taken two rather different lines: either they are feared because they represent weak and debilitating forms of learning experience, or else they are feared because they are machines. Bruno Bettelheim has pointed out that the proper response to these dangers, if not to the criticisms, is not to deny or to neglect the dangers of the situations,

... not to run away from it by destroying it and depriving oneself of its advantages; but to realize the dangers and meet them with conscious action based upon personal decision. This neutralizes the danger, and lets us enjoy the advantages of technology without letting it deprive us of our humanity.

The decision, however, on whether to use a particular learning or teaching resource can only be based upon an analysis of its characteristics and how far it is likely to be useful in realizing the objectives of the system. That is what this book is all about.

I. K. DAVIES
Brampton, England

Introduction

Developing Vocational Instruction is designed to aid both the skilled craftsman who is preparing instruction through which to teach his craft, and the experienced vocational or technical instructor who is interested in improving his present course or finds it necessary to prepare a new one. It is not a dissertation on learning theory or an exposition of educational philosophy. Nor does it prescribe *what* to teach. It is designed to help develop instruction in a vocational or technical field, according to procedures developed in the research laboratory and tested in the classroom. Our assumption is that you are interested in turning out graduates who can perform effectively on the job, and that you are interested in being able to demonstrate your success at doing so.

Teaching is the facilitation of learning. Teaching is warranted to the extent that it causes learning to be more effectively achieved than would have been the case in the absence of instruction. In other words, the main justification for the existence of instruction is that it assists an individual to learn something better than he would by himself. It is the burden of instructors to demonstrate the value of their efforts by demonstrating their ability to facilitate the process of learning. The plumber fails if he cannot stop a leak ... the machinist is useless if he shapes metal but doesn't shape it according to the blueprint ... and the surgeon fails if he operates but removes the wrong part.

So, too, the instructor fails if he goes through all the motions but cannot (or will not) demonstrate that his students can perform according to the course objectives.

Developing Vocational Instruction describes the steps involved in preparing instruction that can be demonstrated to facilitate learning. In so doing, the concern is not with what would be the easiest thing to do, but what will be the most professional. Probably better than anyone else, vocational and technical instructors realize that there can be just as big a difference between practicing a skill and teaching it as there is between teaching and telling. The goal of this book is to describe the steps that must be carried out if one is to become as expert in the skill of systematic course development as he is in the practice of his own vocation or technical specialty.

The procedure of systematic course development outlined in this book is not specific to subject matter or vocation, and it applies to many academic as well as vocational and technical areas.

The original, shorter version of *Developing Vocational Instruction* was prepared pursuant to a contract with the United States Department of Health, Education, and Welfare, Office of Education, under the provisions of Title VII-B of the National Defense Education Act. Points of view or opinions stated do not necessarily represent official Office of Education position or policy.

For reviewing an early draft and offering sound suggestions for improvement, the authors wish to thank Jim Finn, Ben Edelman, Trevor Serviss, Desmond Wedberg, and Lee Cochran, members of the Vocational Education Committee of the Educational Media Council, and Otto Legg and Marvin Feldman. We acknowledge our indebtedness to David Cram and Richard B. Lewis for their detailed critique of the early draft, to Desmond Wedberg for the preparation of the material in Chapter 14, to Bruce Bergum for his critical analysis of ideas—and his patience, and to Ivor Davies for his exceptional preface.

And a deep bow to Elsie Daily and Clarice Kelley, who kept all the horses running in approximately the same direction.

Of course, errors and oversights must be assigned to . . .

R. F. MAGER and K. M. BEACH, JR.

Contents

1 Strategy of Instructional Development

How would you go about setting up a plant to manufacture a particular product? Would you begin by ordering machinery, by setting up a production line, or by hiring personnel? Or would you begin by insisting on seeing a detailed blueprint of the product you intended to produce?

What is usually meant when someone says that he performs his job systematically? Does it mean that he picks a tool at random from his toolbox, that he tries the first thing that comes to his mind, or that he uses the same tool for every job? Or does it mean that he first analyzes the problem, decides exactly what result he wants to obtain, selects and applies the tool most suitable to getting the desired result, and then checks to see that the result has actually been obtained?

The systematic development of instruction is accomplished by a procedure similar to that implied in the paragraph above. It involves detailed specifications of the desired result (in the form of a course graduate); development of an instrument by which success can be measured; development of procedures, lessons, and materials designed to achieve the specified result; and steps to insure the continual improvement of course effectiveness.

1

In this chapter, we will summarize all the steps of the process. In the chapters to follow, we will describe how each of the steps may be accomplished. Some of the steps are easier to perform than others, and some of the steps are more familiar than others. Although some of the steps ask you to do things you may not have done before, the over-all process is one with which you are already familiar. The reason for this is simply that systematic course development is no different than systematic development of an airplane, or systematic design and construction of a building, or systematic performance of the tasks associated with your own profession. *The tools are different, but the procedure is the same.*

Essentially, the three phases of the procedure ask us to:

1. Determine and describe what it is we want to achieve,
2. Do what is necessary to achieve the desired result, and
3. Check to see that we have succeeded in doing what we set out to do.

In developing instruction, this means:

1. Deriving and describing the objectives in meaningful form,
2. Developing lessons and materials designed to meet these objectives and trying out the course, and
3. Determining how well the objectives were achieved and improving the course to improve the results.

Regardless of subject matter, the object of vocational instruction is to send the student away (1) capable of performing satisfactorily on the job and (2) capable of improving his skill through further practice.

To achieve the first goal, it is necessary to know what the job consists of, what one needs to do to perform each of the tasks, and how frequently each of the tasks is performed. The student must be provided with practice in performing these tasks under conditions as much like the job as possible. To reach the second objective (improving skill through performance), it is essential that the student be taught enough about each task so that he can tell the difference between doing it right and doing it wrong (discriminate between perfect performance and imperfect performance), so that he can evaluate his own attempts to perform each of the job tasks. You see, experience is no teacher at all *unless* it is accompanied by information about the accuracy of the performance. Therefore, for the student to be able to improve with practice, it is necessary that he be able to recognize good performance and bad performance when he sees it, whether he sees it in others or in himself.

The strategy of developing effective instruction then, is one that calls for *performance orientation* rather than subject matter orientation. The strategy is to use the job as the basis for deciding what will be taught and in what order and depth, rather than simply to present as much subject matter as possible in the allotted time.

The three phases of course development (shown in Figure 1) include: the preparation phase, the development phase, and the improvement phase. Each phase includes several steps, and a general description of these steps follows. Accomplishment of the steps will be considered in more detail in the following chapters.

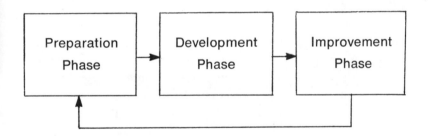

Figure 1. The Phases of Course Development.

Preparation Phase

The steps of the preparation phase (shown in Figure 2) are designed to insure that all the information and practice necessary to perform the job are included in the course. These steps lead to the systematic derivation of course objectives, and begin with the job itself rather than with content.

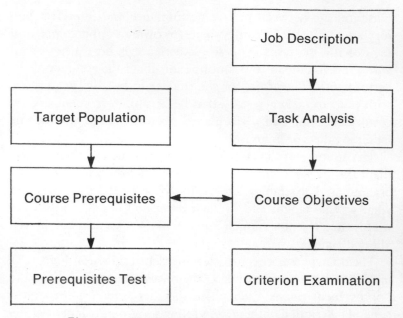

Figure 2. The Steps in Course Preparation.

The first step is describing in general terms that which some-one does when performing the job. The second step is to describe job performance in finer detail, listing each of the tasks of which the job is composed and describing the steps in each of these tasks (task analysis). In the next step the student population is described, as it *exists,* rather than as we would like it to be. Then course prerequisites are prepared, primarily on the basis of the student description, and are adjusted on the basis of the course objectives. Course objectives are derived primarily from task analysis information; they are adjusted on the basis of course prerequisites and such administrative constraints as available time and facilities.

The final step of the preparation phase is that of preparing measuring instruments (examinations) with which to measure success. The criterion exam (similar to final inspection) is de-veloped strictly from the course objectives, and the prerequisites test (entering skill test) is developed strictly from the course prerequisites.

Development Phase

Prerequisites define the starting point . . . objectives define the end point. The difference between what we have (prerequisite skills) and what we want (objectives) is the gap instruction is designed to bridge.

Course development (as shown in Figure 3) begins by outlining instructional units in terms of job tasks so that at the end of *each* unit the student will be able to do something that he couldn't do before, thus helping to insure continued motivation of the student. The next step is to identify the type of performance associated with each of the steps of each of the tasks so that intelligent decisions may be made about instructional techniques most appropriate for the teaching of each task and about selection of instructional materials and devices. Preliminary sequencing of the units is then carried out according to guides intended to maximize student skill and course efficiency. Content is identified, instructional procedures or materials relevant to each lesson are listed, and an appropriate selection is made. Final sequencing is established, lesson plans are completed, and the course is ready for tryout.

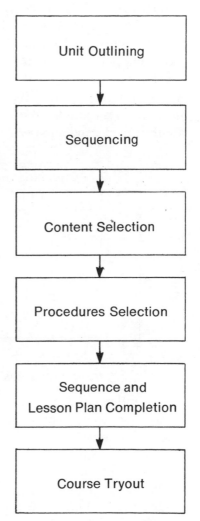

Figure 3. The Steps in Course Development.

Improvement Phase

The professional instructor would no more stop improving his instruction than the professional physician would stop improving his medical skills. Vocations change, new teaching techniques and devices become available, and the average characteristics of the incoming student may gradually shift. It is appropriate, therefore, to set in motion a process guaranteeing that the course will always be as fresh and up-to-date as this morning's newspaper. This is probably the simplest part of the development process, and involves checking to see how well the instruction meets the objectives, and checking to see how the the objectives continue to meet the job. Indicated modifications are then made, and another tryout is conducted (Figure 4).

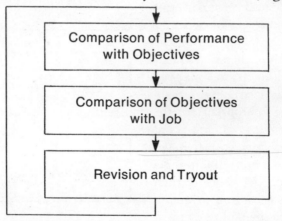

Comparison of Performance
with Objectives

Comparison of Objectives
with Job

Revision and Tryout

Figure 4: The Steps in Course Improvement.

The following pages describe each of the steps above, and provide an assortment of examples. Though the steps are described in sequence, it is not meant to imply that any step is completed and then forever left untouched. In practice it is often necessary to modify what was done in earlier steps in light of what develops in later steps.

One final comment. While the systematic development of instruction is a specific procedure that can be described in detail, the procedure is not specific to subject matter or vocations. Regardless of the intent of the instruction, the procedure for developing the course is basically the same.

2 Job Description

From the very beginning of the course development process, it is appropriate to adopt a job-oriented point of view so that only the most relevant subject matter and learning activities are built into the course.

The first step of the preparation phase, therefore, is to locate, or write, a job description. A job description is a general statement about what a person on the job does, and tells something about the conditions under which he does them. It is NOT a description of what he *knows*. A job description is generally only a paragraph or two long.

If you cannot locate a job description, write one. Think about doing the job, and list the various tasks that are involved. Also list any special or unusual conditions under which the task is carried out. For example, a description of the plumber's job would probably indicate that he often has to work in confined places and in his customer's houses; a radio announcer has to work under time pressure; and a waiter is expected to be polite to his customers.

One note of caution. It is important to include ALL classes of things that are done on the job, even though they don't relate to the basic skill. If, for example, the job you will be teaching is that of auto mechanic, and if the mechanic on the job is required to fill out certain forms or to do other paper work, include that fact in the job description. If the man on the job is expected to give an occasional guided tour through the work area, include that. A job description describes the job *as it is* ... not as you would like it to be.

Example 1

Vocation: Machinist

The machinist is a skilled metal worker who shapes metal or nonmetal parts by using machine and hand tools. He is able to select the proper tools and materials required for each job, and to plan the cutting, bending, etc., and finishing operations in their proper order so that he can complete the finished work according to blueprint or written specifications. He is able to interpret blueprints and read precision measuring instruments. He is able to convert fractional values into decimal equivalents.

The machinist is able to set up and operate most types of machine tools. He selects the appropriate machine and cutting tools that will turn raw material into an intricate, precise part.

Example 2

Vocation: Radio and Television Service Technician

A radio and television service technician may be required to install, maintain, and service amplitude and frequency modulated home and auto receivers, transistorized radios, monochrome and color television systems, high fidelity amplifiers, and tape recorders. He is able to read circuit diagrams and codes of values and to select component substitutes.

The radio and television service technician's work requires meeting the public both in the repair shop and on service calls. In order to service home receivers or equipment, he may be required to drive a car or truck. He must be able to tolerate heights, as antenna installations on rooftops are often an everyday occurrence. A service technician who establishes his own business may need to know how to maintain business records and inventory.

Example 3

Vocation: Welder

The welder possesses a great deal of manipulative skill both in the art of welding and in jig preparation. He is skilled in blueprint reading and has some knowledge of metallurgy. He is able to join two pieces of metal to form one precision part by arc, gas, or spot welding. He is able to specify the type of metal that will most likely meet blueprint specifications. Since there are many ways to weld, he is able to select the method that will yield a satisfactory finished product.

In addition to understanding the principles of welding, the welder is able to operate sheet metal tools. He is able to shear, brake, and manipulate sheet metal before joining. He is also experienced in silver and lead soldering techniques. In essence, he is able to construct, join, and finish two pieces of metal according to blueprint specifications and to repair broken or perforated members.

Example 4

Vocation: Landscape Gardener

A landscape gardener has knowledge of lawns, shrubs, annual and perennial flowers, pest and disease control, soil structure, fertility, and other information that enables him to plant and maintain beautiful landscapes. He provides a service in the area of design, selection, and maintenance of most plant life. He possesses fundamental knowledge of the methods of propagation by seeding, grafting, layering, and cutting. He is an expert in taxonomy. He is acquainted with the various plant diseases and physiology. He is able to provide sketches of landscaping design to various clients to meet their specifications. He is often required to supervise nonskilled helpers.

The job requires that he be able to drive a truck, meet customers, and be acquainted with and operate manual equipment. During the off-season, he may be required to participate in tree surgery or other forms of work related to his job. He is often required to keep systematic charts showing planting areas and maintain customer records pertaining to plant maintenance or rotation.

Example 5

Vocation: X-ray Technician

An X-ray technician X-rays healthy, sick, and disabled people without regard to race, creed, or color. He performs his work either in a hospital, a clinic, a private office, or an industrial environment. He has a working knowledge of human bone structures, X-ray equipment selection and maintenance, film processing, and nursing skills. He must be able to adjust to any situation, whether routine or emergency, and X-ray a patient both quickly and efficiently. He is usually on call twenty-four hours a day.

The X-ray technician must be neat in appearance and work habits. Since he deals with the sick and disabled, he must be tolerant and considerate of their condition.

The job description is adequate when it contains a comment about *each* of the kinds of activities a person engages in during his performance of the job, and when it suggests the special or unusual conditions associated with the performance of the job.

3 Task Analysis

The job description sketches the outlines and "high spots" of the job to be taught, but isn't a good enough basis from which to develop a course. It isn't specific enough, and so the task analysis is the next step.

A task is a logically related set of actions required for the completion of a job objective. Stated another way, a task is a complete job element. A job or vocation includes a number of tasks. For example, one of the tasks that must be performed by the auto mechanic is that of changing a tire; all of the steps involved in tire changing go to make up the complete task. One part of the salesman's job is writing orders; that is *one task* that makes up the salesman's *job*. Preparing a batch of mortar is one task making up the mason's job.

Task Listing

The *first step* in the task analysis is listing *all* the tasks that might be included in the job. You can probably list most of them just by thinking about the job awhile and by looking at your job description. But you will do a better job if you do not stop there. Talk with individuals now working at the job, or watch them actually doing the job. This will help refresh your memory, and help you to avoid a serious teaching trap... loading the course with irrelevant content.

Talking with the man on the job will tell you what the job *is*. Talking to the supervisor will tell you what it *ought* to be. You will have to use your judgment as to which tasks are reasonable to include in your list based on probability of need.

A note of caution. You will not be teaching all of the tasks you list in your analysis. Some will be deleted for reasons we will explain later. But the important thing is to list *all* the tasks that go to make up the vocation.

Here are two examples of what such a list might look like. The first is taken from Harless.*

Example 1

Vocation: Service Station Mechanic-attendant

1. Cleans or replaces spark plugs.
2. Adjusts and bleeds brakes.
3. Replaces wheel cylinders.
4. Inspects and flushes radiators.
5. Tests antifreeze.
6. Repairs tube or tubeless tires.
7. Rotates tires.
8. Lubricates vehicles.
9. Balances tires.
10. Replaces air cleaners.
11. Cleans or replaces gas filters.
12. Washes and waxes autos.
13. Sells auto accessories.
14. Replaces oil filters.
15. Checks oil, brake fluid, power steering, etc.
16. Washes windshields, replaces blades.
17. Fills gas tanks, radiators.
18. Keeps daily records of sales, inventory changes.
19. Orders supplies.
20. Opens and closes station.

Example 2

Vocation: Painter

1. Refinishes old as well as new surfaces.
2. Selects paint, varnish, lacquer, or other types of finishing material.

*J. H. Harless, "The Ugly Duckling Learns To Fly," *NSPI Journal,* 1966, Vol. 5, pp. 3-6.

3. Selects appropriate brushes and rollers.
4. Removes trim and obstacles before finishing.
5. Removes existing finish from surfaces when appropriate.
6. Fills cracks and holes with appropriate substitutes.
7. Mixes and thins finishing material to correct consistency.
8. Adds color to finishing material when necessary.
9. Masks areas not to be finished.
10. Selects and supplies appropriate ground and furniture covering.
11. Operates a "ladder" truck.
12. Countersinks nails, brads, and other obstructions.
13. Waxes, and replaces doors, drawers, etc., when finished.
14. Acts as a consultant to the public.
15. Cleans area when finished.
16. Orders supplies.
17. Maintains records of previous jobs, colors, and materials.

It will be useful to list all these tasks on a simple form so that you can easily record the information you need to put down next. As you can see by the sample form (Figure 5), there are three columns to the right of the place where each task is listed. The first column is headed "Frequency of Performance," and is where you should indicate how *often* each task is performed during the performance of the job. When filling out this column, try not to think about whether the task is important or unimportant; just indicate the frequency with which the task is performed. Use a recording scheme that fits your own subject matter; for some occupations it is reasonable to write down the number of times a particular task is performed each day, each week, or maybe even each month. Whether you record the actual number of times a task is performed during some given length of time, or whether you merely indicate whether the task is performed frequently, once in awhile, or very rarely, this information will become very useful in deciding how deeply to go into the subject, how much practice to provide, and how to sequence the course lessons.

All tasks are not of equal importance in the performance of a job. Tasks that are performed frequently may not represent a critical skill. Other tasks, although performed rarely, are vital to job performance. For example: Although a waiter must know how to clean off a table and may perform this task frequently, it is not nearly as important to the job as his ability to take

TASK LISTING SHEET

Vocation: _____

No.	Task	Frequency of Performance	Impor-tance	Learning Difficulty

Figure 5.

13

customers' orders correctly. Under the column headed "Importance," indicate the relative importance of the task in the practice of the vocation. Label each task 1, 2, or 3 to indicate your judgment of importance. Then, you will be able to determine which tasks must be included in the training and which can be left out if some selection becomes necessary.

The third column of the form is labeled "Learning Difficulty," and is a column you should fill in while looking yourself straight in the eye (which is a neat trick without a mirror). Here your best estimate is required of whether each task is easy to learn, moderately difficult to learn, or very difficult to learn. The accuracy with which you can make these judgments is largely influenced by how long it is since you yourself learned the tasks. If you recently learned to perform these tasks, you are a good judge of their learning difficulty; if it has been quite a while since you learned them, it would be wise to consult with a student or two. As you well know, people who can do things well frequently forget how difficult it was to learn to do them.

Another note of caution. The purpose of a form is to make a task easier. If the forms we offer as aids do not facilitate your recording the details of the tasks you will be teaching, change them to fit your needs. Do not distort your description of the job just to fit the forms. On page 15 is an example of what your Task Listing Sheet might look like when completely filled out.

Task Detailing

The *second step* in the task analysis is to list the steps involved in each of the tasks on the list in terms of what the person *does* when performing the step. If this step is left out, it is possible to fall into one of two teaching traps. One is the trap of spending a lot of time teaching something that is difficult to teach, even though it is not one of the highly important things to teach. That is, it is possible to spend more and more time teaching a difficult but relatively unimportant topic.

The other trap is that of forgetting to include in the course something that is very easy to teach but that is absolutely essential to learn. For example, it is essential that a missile repairman

TASK LISTING SHEET

Vocation: Electronics Technician

No.	Task	Frequency of Performance	Importance	Learning Difficulty
1.	Troubleshoots and repairs malfunctioning equipment.	Everyday occurrence	1	Difficult
2.	Reads electronic schematics.	1 to 10 times a day	2	Moderate
3.	Performs chassis layouts.	Once a week	2	Easy
4.	Uses small hand tools.	Continuously	1	Easy
5.	Checks electronic components.	Frequently	1	Moderate to very difficult
6.	Replaces components.	Once in a while	2	Easy to moderate
7.	Solders various components.	Frequently	2	Moderate
8.	Recognizes the applicability of electronic test equipment.	Once in a while	2	Difficult
9.	Interprets test instruments.	Frequently	1	Difficult
10.	Performs calibration of test equipment.	Once a month	3	Difficult
11.	Interprets and records test data.	Once in a while	3	Easy to moderate
12.	Specifies and orders electronic components.	Frequently	3	Easy
13.	Applies first aid procedures.	Very rarely	1	Moderate
14.	Maintains and cleans work areas.	Frequently	2	Easy

15

be able to locate each of the units he might be expected to work on (he can't fix it if he can't find it). Since the location of parts is such a simple thing to teach, one course we know of simply assumed that the student "couldn't possibly get through the course without learning the location of the units." The fact is, though, that the students could, and did, graduate without being able to find many of the things they would be expected to repair. By knowing in detail what the job involves, it is less likely that essential but easy to teach items will be accidentally left out of the course.

The second step in the task analysis, then, is to list each of the steps involved in performing each of the tasks in terms of what is *done*, rather than in terms of what must be known. Following are some examples of tasks that have been broken down into their main steps.

Example 1

Vocation: Electronics Technician

Task: Soldering components

1. Identify joint to be soldered.
2. Select the appropriate iron and solder.
3. Clean joint and tin if necessary.
4. Place the iron on the joint.
5. Apply the appropriate amount of rosin core solder to the joint.
6. Check and examine the joint; seal if necessary.
7. Clean surroundings and replace tools when finished.

Example 2

Vocation: Service Station Mechanic-attendant

Task: Clean and replace air filter

1. Identify the type of cleaner to be used.
2. Remove filter assembly.
3. Drain and clean cartridge and filter holder.
4. Refill bowl with clean oil.
5. Reassemble unit into mount.
6. Check for performance.
7. Clean area and replace tools.

Example 3

Vocation: Service Station Mechanic-attendant

Task: Clean and replace spark plugs

1. Note plug location relative to the cylinder; remove plug covers, leads.
2. Remove all spark plugs.
3. Identify the type of plugs.
4. Decide whether to clean, adjust, and/or replace plugs.
5. Adjust and clean plugs, if appropriate.
6. Reinsert plugs in engine.
7. Connect ignition wire to appropriate plugs.
8. Check engine firing for maximum performance.
9. Clean and replace equipment and tools.

Example 4

Vocation: Painter

Task: Refinishes wood

1. Identify the type of wood to be refinished.
2. Select appropriate paint or finish remover.
3. Remove old finish with appropriate remover.
4. Sand and fill where necessary.
5. Apply stain, sealer, or other agent.
6. Apply finish coat of lacquer, paint, varnish, or some other finishing agent.
7. Smooth and polish when dry.
8. Repeat steps above as often as required for quality finish.
9. Check for color, smoothness, and completeness.
10. Clean work area and equipment.

Here again, we can offer some help to make the job of task detailing easier. Each task has some steps in common. For example: The skilled craftsman needs to be able to recognize *if* a task needs to be performed, and he must be able to recognize *when* he has performed the task correctly or successfully. These are important aspects of every task and must not be neglected in the design of the course.

Beyond that, there are some steps that may or may not be part of a task, such as knowing (being able to list) the proper sequence of steps to be performed.

To help you as a memory aid, here are some steps that might be included in the performance of a task:

- Recognize when to perform the task.
- Select appropriate tools and materials.
- Locate the correct objects on which to work.
- Perform the safety procedures associated with the task.
- Check work.

Some of the steps often included in the performance of a task, but which are not *visible* while they are being performed, are these:

- Identify the sequence of steps that must be followed to perform the task correctly.
- Describe how . . . . works.
- Describe the theory of why . . . . works.
- Recognize dangers associated with performing the task.
- Recognize the differences between a properly performed task and an improperly performed task.

The Task Detailing Sheet (Figure 6) should prove helpful in completing the second part of the task analysis. Once again, you are advised to adjust the form to the task situation rather than force the facts to fit the form.

After the steps in each task have been listed, it is appropriate to fill in the two remaining columns on the detailing sheet (one sheet for each task). Since it is likely that identification of the type of learning involved in each step will be new to you, that will be discussed in a chapter to follow. At the moment, we will say only that the information in that column will be of critical importance in deciding which teaching technique is appropriate at each step.

The column labeled "Learning Difficulty" is similar to the one on the sheet on which you have listed all the tasks. There is one difference, however. It is very likely that the student will already be able to perform some of the steps when he arrives for instruction. As we do not want to bore the student by teaching him what he already knows, we will want him to perform the things he can *already* do *only* when he is asked to perform the

TASK DETAILING SHEET

Vocation: _____

Task: _____

No.	*Steps in Performing the Task*	*Type of Performance*	*Learning Difficulty*

Figure 6.

19

entire task; we will not teach him these steps separately. Thus, whenever a step is found that the student is very likely to be able to perform, put a special mark in the learning difficulty column. For the remaining items, indicate whether they are easy to learn, of moderate difficulty, or difficult to learn.

While this may seem to be going into unnecessary detail, it must be stressed that these steps are essential in making intelligent choices of teaching techniques. With the task steps identified in this detail, we can better avoid the teaching trap of including more theory than is necessary or desirable, and keep the course performance oriented. Without this detail, we might add hours or days of unnecessary theory, as was the case in a radar course for which a task analysis was not prepared. This course included a four-hour block of lectures on the theory of wave guides. A wave guide is a piece of metal pipe that serves the same function as a piece of wire, and there is absolutely nothing that can be done with a piece that becomes badly dented or for some other reason malfunctions . . . except to replace it.

Since the object of the course was to develop men who could repair the radar when it developed trouble, lectures on the theory of wave guide construction were completely useless and irrelevant . . . and served merely to bore and confuse the student. When the managers of the course finally developed detailed objectives based on a task analysis, these lectures were eliminated.

There are probably as many techniques for performing a task analysis as there are people doing it. The technique described here, while not nearly as detailed as some, is adequate for the job at hand. If you know of another technique that suits you better, by all means use it. The only large error you can make is not to use any task analysis technique at all.

Following are four examples of completed Task Detailing Sheets.

TASK DETAILING SHEET

Vocation: Service Station Mechanic-attendant

Task: Clean and replace spark plugs

No.	Steps in Performing the Task	Type of Performance	Learning Difficulty
1.	Note the plug location relative to the cylinder.	Recall	Easy
2.	Remove all spark plugs.	Manipulation	Easy
3.	Identify the type of plugs.	Discrimination	✓
4.	Decide whether to adjust or replace plugs.	Problem-solving	Moderately difficult
5.	Clean plugs, if necessary.	Manipulation	✓
6.	Adjust plugs, if appropriate.	Manipulation	Moderately difficult
7.	Replace spark plugs in engine.	Manipulation	✓
8.	Connect ignition wires to appropriate plugs.	Recall, manipulation	Moderately difficult
9.	Check for performance.	Discrimination	Very difficult
10.	Clean tools and equipment.	Manipulation	✓

Note that some of these steps cannot be seen directly, but that they are nonetheless important in completing the task.

TASK DETAILING SHEET

Vocation: X-ray Technician

Task: Take an X-ray of the chest

No.	Steps in Performing the Task	Type of Performance	Learning Difficulty
1.	Patient is asked to prepare for the X-ray by removing excess clothing.	Speech	Easy
2.	Correctly position the patient, giving special instructions.	Manipulation, speech	Moderately difficult
3.	Position and check the proper distance of the tube with respect to the patient.	Discrimination	Moderately difficult
4.	Turn on the X-ray equipment and adjust machine.	Recall	Easy
5.	Insert the X-ray film and identification marker into the proper holder.	Manipulation	Easy
6.	Expose film and release patient from examining room.	Manipulation	Moderately difficult
7.	Process film.	Manipulation	Difficult
8.	Check film for specified positioning or developing errors.	Discrimination	Very difficult
9.	Release patient if film is acceptable to the radiologist.	Recall	√
10.	Clean examining table and film areas.	Manipulation	√

TASK DETAILING SHEET

Vocation: Arborist

Task: Pruning of a shade tree

No.	Steps in Performing the Task	Type of Performance	Learning Difficulty
1.	Note the location of the tree with respect to utility wires, buildings, and pertinent surroundings.	Discrimination	Easy
2.	Inspect the tree for diseases and insect manifestations.	Discrimination	Very difficult
3.	Examine the tree for dead, broken, or weak limbs.	Discrimination	Moderately difficult
4.	Begin by removing branches that are in contact with one another, starting at the top and working toward the base.	Manipulation	Easy
5.	Examine and proceed to remove all dead material or abnormal growth.	Manipulation	Easy
6.	Trim balance of tree by clipping small growths at the junction of main branches; large growths, by cutting parallel to the trunk.	Manipulation	Moderately difficult
7.	Paint all major cuts.	Recall	Easy
8.	Brace weakened structures to avoid splitting.	Recall	Moderately difficult
9.	Shape tree to desired crown.	Manipulation	Very difficult
10.	Observe results, repeating steps above, if necessary.	Discrimination	Difficult
11.	Remove cuttings.	Recall	✓
12.	Clean and sharpen tools.	Manipulation	✓

23

TASK DETAILING SHEET

Vocation: Hairdresser

Task: Hairstyling

No.	Steps in Performing the Task	Type of Performance	Learning Difficulty
1.	Select suitable hairstyles on the basis of hair color, head shape, and facial contour.	Discrimination, recall	Very difficult
2.	Discuss proposed styles with client and obtain agreement.	Problem-solving	Easy
3.	Shape from nape of neck toward both ears, using scissors and comb, moving toward crown.	Manipulation	Very difficult
4.	Brush loose hair away as needed.	Manipulation	✓
5.	Separate hair using comb and clips.	Manipulation	Easy
6.	Shape left side of head until desired length is reached.	Manipulation	Moderately difficult
7.	Shape right side of head until desired length is reached.	Manipulation	Moderately difficult
8.	Style by trimming, combing, and brushing.	Manipulation	Moderately difficult
9.	Check work to see that hair is consistently shaped to the desired style.	Discrimination	Easy
10.	Remove all loose hair from client.	Manipulation	✓
11.	Repeat steps above as needed.	Manipulation	✓
12.	Sterilize tools and clean area in preparation for the next client.	Manipulation	Easy

4 Target Population

Although the design of a vocational course is strongly influenced by a careful analysis of the vocation itself, it is also influenced by the kind of students who show up for training. The course must be designed for the target population (students) that acually exists. It is foolish and wasteful to design a course without defining the target population. The major characteristics of the target population constitute the starting point of the course, the performance called for in the course objectives constitutes the finishing point, and the process of turning the incoming student into the skilled graduate constitutes the course itself. In other words, the substance of the course is derived *by subtracting what the student already is able to do from what you want him to be able to do.*

Suppose a stranger asked you to tell him about the students you have, or expect to have, in one of your courses. What would you tell him? The things you tell him in answer to this question are the things you should write down when beginning your description of the target population. Some of the categories about which you might want to comment are as follows:

1. *Physical characteristics.* The physical nature of your students may influence the tools and procedures that can be included in the instruction. Describe the general nature of your population; indicate general handicaps as well as assets such as special strength, agility, balance, or endurance.

2. *Education.*   The kind of education your incoming students have had in the past will have a good deal of influence on the length of the course, examples you can use, vocabulary that will be understood, and the level of abstraction that might be meaningful.

3. *Motivation.*   Are the students generally eager to learn the occupation you are teaching, or is motivation something of a problem? The less motivated you feel they are, the more you will have to concern yourself with keeping students interested at every step of the course.

4. *Interests.*   What kinds of things *are* the students interested in? Knowing their interests will help keep them motivated. What are their special skills or aptitudes? Are they good at fixing cars? Are they short on manual dexterity? The answers to these questions will assist you in writing realistic prerequisites, and may have some influence on what you can reasonably expect in the way of terminal performance from your students.

5. *Attitudes, biases, and prejudices.*   Does your target population consist primarily of one ethnic group? What are their strong convictions and biases? This information may also influence the kind of examples you can effectively use, and may provide other clues to student motivation.

Example 1

Physical characteristics . . . Female; 18-40 years of age.

Education . . . . Average of two years of college, above-average intelligence.

Motivation   . . . . Desire to learn a skill relative to husbands occupations. Husbands are scientists and engineers.

Interests . . . . Civic activities, local politics. They attend local lectures and are active in garden and art clubs.

Attitudes, biases, and
prejudices . . . . They prefer to associate with educated people. Like to think of themselves as educated, but would rather tend to their clubs than to their children.

Example 2

Physical characteristics . . . Male; 12-20 years old; physically strong, good stamina.

Education . . . . High school dropouts; generally below-average intelligence. Few have been outside the county in which they were born. Know simple arithmetic operations, but cannot calculate rapidly or perform any algebraic operations. There is good knowledge of how simple machines work.

Motivation . . . . Desire recognition, wheels, and women.

Interests . . . . They like to work with their hands; show good mechanical dexterity. Prefer to work outdoors most of the time. Interests are limited to immediate neighborhood and the things around them.

Attitudes, biases, and
prejudices . . . . Students live in a poor environment and are suspicious of everyone not exactly like themselves. They hate everything about school. Prejudice about race and nationality is deep and widespread, but they are friendly and like to have fun. Abhor waste, and can make do with very little.

Summaries such as these provide a place to start in the description of the target population. But something more is required . . . information about specific knowledge relevant to the subject of the course. What do incoming students know that will make learning the subject easy? What do they know, or not know, that will make learning difficult? For example: If the student will have to handle instruments of various kinds, does he already know how to read scales? Does he know how to interpret scales? If so, that is a help. If not, these skills will have to be taught.

The more you know about the target population, the more accurately you will be able to derive the content of the course . . . the more accurately you will be able to subtract what is known from what needs to be known.

What needs to be known? How shall we derive the objectives of the course so that the target of instruction shall be clearly visible? This step is discussed in the next chapter.

5 Course Objectives

recent majo renslish to repeat the new
performante-the real-portion the test of job

All information is now available with which to construct the most important document ... the blueprint of student performance you want to develop. This blueprint is essential because it will describe what the student is expected to be like at the time he leaves the course—at the time, in other words, that he leaves your influence. It is important because it is the document from which one prepares the measuring instrument (criterion examination) by which decisions can be made about the adequacy or inadequacy of student performance. It is important because when a modified version is given to the student he will be better able to organize his own activities and efforts leading him to the kind of performance you want to see. It is important because it will provide a document you can use to demonstrate your systematic development of instruction, and that can be used in response to uninformed criticisms about procedures you are using in the course.

The statement of course objectives consists of as many statements, items, or examples as are necessary to describe the desired behavior of the student at the time he leaves the course. It is prepared in enough detail so another professional instructor could turn out a student who could do the kinds of things *you* want him to do at the proficiency levels you desire.

Course objectives differ from the task analysis in several ways. The task analysis describes the vocation or job as it is performed by a highly skilled person. Objectives describe the kind of performance that will be expected at the end of the course. For example: While a highly skilled person may be able to perform a particular machine adjustment in five or ten seconds without using any job aids to remind him of the steps, it might be unrealistic to expect a course graduate to perform that well on the day of graduation. It might be far more realistic to expect the new graduate to be able to perform the task without the use of job aids in ten or fifteen minutes. *If* he can perform all of the steps of the job, and *if* he can determine when the job is properly performed, *then* practice on the job will improve his proficiency.

The task analysis describes all of the steps carried out in the performance of the job, whether or not the student knows how to perform some of these steps before he enters the course. The objectives of the course differ from the task analysis in that they do not include those things that the student already knows.

Another difference between task analysis and course objectives is in the subject matter itself. It may be that some of the skills called for in performing an occupation are either unrealistic to teach in the classroom or are better taught on the job. An example of this might be the paper work expected of a skilled craftsman. This task is likely to be so different from one location to another, and so easy to teach (relatively speaking), that it might be a task better learned on the job.

The key question to ask is this: *What kind of things should the student be able to do at the end of the course that will most facilitate his becoming a skilled craftsman in the least amount of time?* In other words, what should the student be able to do at the end of the course so that all that stands between the student and skilled performance is practice?

Course objectives represent a clear statement of instructional intent, and are written in any form necessary to clarify that intent. In practice, you will have at *least* twice as many statements as you have tasks on your list. These statements will have the following characteristics:

1. An objective says something about the student. It does not describe the textbook, the instructor, or the kinds of classroom experience to which the student will be exposed.

2. An objective talks about the behavior or performance of students. It does not describe the performance of the teacher, nor does it describe what the student is expected to know or understand. Though you might begin an objective by a general statement such as, "the student must understand the operation of the XYZ sewing machine," you would go on to explain what you mean by understanding by describing what the student will be expected to do to demonstrate your definition of understanding. In some cases the student may be expected to answer questions, or to solve some problems, or to describe a procedure, or to construct a gadget. Whatever it is *you* mean by understanding would be defined in the sentences to follow the general one. In any case, an objective describes what the *student* will be *doing* to demonstrate his achievement of your instructional intent.

3. An objective is about ends rather than means. It describes a product rather than a process. As such, it describes what the student is expected to be like at the end of instruction rather than the means that will be used to get him there. It talks about terminal performance rather than course content.

4. An objective describes the conditions under which the student will be performing his terminal behavior. In some cases the student will be expected to perform in the absence of any assistance provided by job aids; in some cases, such aids are acceptable. For example: Sometimes the student may be expected to solve problems with the use of a slide rule or calculator, and sometimes without these items.

5. An instructional objective also includes information about the level of performance that will be considered acceptable. If a student will be expected to perform a task within five

minutes at the end of the course, this will be stated as part of the objective. If his performance at the end of the course is expected to be error-free or if some error will be tolerated, this would be indicated. In most instances, the decision about what performance will be considered acceptable is an arbitrary one. This is one place where the experience and wisdom of the instructor is most important, because specification of satisfactory performance is one of the unique contributions that can be made only by the skilled instructor.

For convenience, it is possible to classify objectives into two broad categories, those that describe specific performances of the student and those that may be needed to describe his attitudes. For example: If it is important to send the student away more interested in the subject than he was when he arrived, this must be stated in an objective so that the course may be systematically organized to achieve it. If the student will be expected to perform with persistence, then the nature of this persistence should be spelled out so that the course may be designed to achieve this end. It may be that when the student is performing the job each failure on his part will be expected to result in another immediate attempt, as is often the case in jobs involving repair of equipment. If one attempt at fixing fails, another attempt is expected. In other words, each failure experience is expected to trigger another attempt to succeed. Unless this persistence objective is made explicit, it is possible that the procedures used during instruction will turn out a student who will give up after one or two attempts. (And this is just what will happen if, for instance, the instructor makes critical comments following every student attempt to come into contact with the very equipment he is expected to master.)

On some jobs it is important that a pleasant tone of voice be used, as well as a patient manner. When this is the case, it is important to specify this objective and design for its achievement. Most people do not know whether others perceive them as sounding pleasant or patient; this requires instruction. But such instruction may fail to be included in the curriculum unless the objective is made explicit.

In any case, it is important to describe as comprehensively as possible what the student is intended to be like when he leaves the course.

On the pages that follow are some examples of a variety of objectives. Notice that each is relatively specific and deals with either a single task or with steps within a task. Notice that each tells what the student will be doing when he is demonstrating that he has achieved the objective, and that each says something about what will be considered as acceptable performance. Some are stated in a single sentence; others are wordier. The form isn't the important thing, *what is important is that instructional intent be made clear.*

Example 1

Given an unfinished metal casting, be able to surface, drill, and tap according to the specifications indicated on the attached blueprint.

Example 2

Provided with an outdoor television antenna kit and appropriate tools, be able to install the antenna and correctly connect the input lead to the television set. Performance will be judged correct if the antenna installation is completed according to trade standards and if the resulting TV picture is free of snow.

Example 3

Given a model XYZ sphygmomanometer, be able to take blood pressure to within 0.05 cm. The student must correctly complete five consecutive trials to this criterion.

Example 4

    Goal: Be able to point out forest fire hazards in a forest area.
Behavior: Identify dangerous conditions by pointing.
                Conditions: The student must have access to forest areas and be exposed to dangerous conditions determined by the instructor.
                Criterion: The student must identify nine out of ten danger areas identified by the instructor.
                Criterion: Given a descriptive list of dangerous suitations, rank order them according to most to least dangerous.

Example 5

Goal: Be familiar with technical terms commonly used in nursing.
Behavior: Match term with correct definition.
             Conditions: Given list of terms and definitions.
              Criterion: 8 correct matches out of 10.
Criterion Test Item: Here is a list of . . .
Behavior: State meaning of sentence containing term "diastolic."
             Conditions: Given a sentence containing the word "diastolic."
                Criteria: Essential elements—rhythmic recurrence, expansion, dilation of heart cavities.
Criterion Test Item: Please read the following sentence . . .

Example 6

To be able to transcribe a business letter from a dictating machine of the following type (model indicated here) and be able to produce a typed letter with a minimum of three typing errors, with all typing errors corrected.

No doubt you noticed that these objectives do not all take the same form. Two consist of a single sentence, and two others are made up of two or more sentences. Two consist of a general statement followed by statements intended to clarify the nature of acceptable performance. Objectives should take whatever form will help make the instructional intent clear.

For a thorough discussion of objectives, and for further examples of the different kinds of objectives that might be written, the following references are recommended:

1. Bloom, B. S. (ed.); Engelhart, M. D.; Furst, E. H.; Hill, W. H.; and Krathwohl, D. R. *Taxonomy of Educational Objectives. Handbook I: Cognitive Domain.* New York: David McKay, 1956.
2. Krathwohl, D. R.; Bloom, B. S.; and Masia, B. B. *Taxonomy of Educational Objectives. Handbook II: Affective Domain.* New York: David McKay, 1964.
3. Mager, R. F. *Preparing Instructional Objectives.* Palo Alto, Calif.: Fearon Publishers, 1962.

To prepare your own objectives, use your task analysis sheets as your guide. You might find it most convenient to write a task at the top of a sheet and then beneath it describe in more detail what the student will be expected to do at the end of the course in relation to that task. If that technique doesn't appeal to you, here is another used by some instructors. A sheet of paper is divided into three columns and a general objective statement is put in the left-hand column. The center column is used to describe the conditions (givens, constraints, etc.) under which the student will be expected to perform, and the third column is used to describe what the student will be doing to demonstrate his achievement of the objective.

As is true with the other steps in systematic course development, each step is not completed and then forgotten. Objectives are written before the course is prepared, but they are continually modified as experience reveals gaps, unrealistic expectations, or other ways in which they may be improved. But the statement of objectives is the key document to performance of all the remaining steps of course development. It is the blueprint describing the skills and performances we hope to achieve in our students. It is a description of the goal we intend to reach. Unless we know precisely where we are going, we might wind up someplace else . . . and never even know it.

With objectives in hand, you have established what you want the student to be like at the time your influence over him comes to an end. You have pinned down the endpoint and know what you want to achieve. But not everyone in the world is qualified to reach such a level of achievement . . . within the time likely to be available for instruction. And the nature of the persons accepted for the course will have an effect on the design of instruction. It is time, therefore, to specify the prerequisite behaviors that will be required for entry into the course.

6 Course Prerequisites

Who will be allowed to enter your course?

Will incoming students be expected to be within certain age limits, be able to read at a certain rate, be able to perform certain mathematical operations, or be able to operate certain machines? The answers to these questions determine the pre- requisites for the course, and the prerequisites will exert some influence on the length of the course and on the need to arrange for remedial instruction.

The fewer the restrictions on the entering student, the larger the number of people who will qualify for the course. But at the same time, the fewer the restrictions, the more necessary it will be to design the course to provide individualized instruction, since students are likely to be quite different from one another in what they can do when they enter.

The more restrictions you place on the entering student, the more likely it is that students can progress as a group. This is not to say that students *ought* to progress as a group, only that they may be more able to do so if they are very similar in background and skills.

The more restrictions that are placed on the entering student, however, the less likely it is that you will find people described by your prerequisites actually existing in the world. The trick is to write prerequisites that are realistic.

The development of realistic prerequisites is not accomplished in a single step; prerequisites grow as other steps of course development are carried out. A useful procedure for the development of course prerequisites is to keep a sheet of paper labeled "Prerequisites" on the wall in front of you while developing the course. Every time you find yourself making an assumption about what you will expect the student to know or be able to do when he enters the course, write that assumption down on the prerequisites sheet. If you are going to *assume* that the student can perform something, turn that assumption into a prerequisite. If you are *not* going to assume he can do it, add it to the course objectives.

As you have probably guessed, we consider absolutely worthless a prerequisite statement that merely gives the name of some course that the student will be expected to have completed. Such a statement is an administrative device that has nothing to do with systematic course development. It provides no information on which to base intelligent decisions.

If you develop your prerequisites as you go, you will be less likely to fall into the teaching trap of imposing irrelevant restrictions, because this is an area where common sense doesn't always coincide with reality. For example: One electronics maintenance course we know of had a prerequisite calling for normal color vision. "Common sense" implied that this was reasonable. After all, some electronic components are color coded, as are some of the wires used in the equipment. The fact of the matter was, however, that several color-blind students completed the course quite successfully. They had no difficulty performing all of the tasks required of them, because no task required that color-coded components be read. The mistake here was that the prerequisite was based on course content rather than on course objectives. Since the content included color-coded items, it seemed reasonable that the student should be able to discriminate among these colors. But the tasks the student was called on to perform didn't require that he be able to discriminate among these colors; hence, a color-blind individual performed just as well as one with normal color vision.

The development of course prerequisites, then, is done with the description of the target population and the objectives rather than with subject matter. For each skill you decide the student must have at the *end* of the course, you must decide whether you will assume that the incoming student already has that skill or not. If you assume that he does, write this assumption on your prerequisites sheet. If you assume that he doesn't, add it to your objectives. Use your target population description to check the realism of your prerequisites. If your prerequisites begin to describe a population of students that is quite different from those you have said you are likely to get, some adjustments are called for. Perhaps some of the prerequisites should be turned into objectives. The realism of your target population description can be checked by testing some students to determine what they can and cannot do when they enter the course.

To give you some idea about how this is done, we will let you in on the stream of thinking we recently went through while deriving a prerequisite for instruction designed to develop electronic technicians.

Let's see, now. One of the things we want the student to be able to do at the end of the course is to interpret waveforms on the oscilloscope. O.K., we'll write that down on our sheet of objectives.

Now what will we assume he can do when he enters the course? We'll assume that he knows how to convert kilocycles to megacycles, for one thing. So we'll write that down on the sheet of prerequisites. O.K., now we know he should be able to make some conversions in order to qualify for the course.

Better check that out by looking at the description of the target population ... oh, oh, that won't do at all. The target population consists of students who haven't finished high school. It is a sure bet they don't know how to make the conversions we just assumed they could do. Let's scratch that prerequisite ... too unrealistic.

Suppose we assume they can add, subtract, multiply, and divide. Can we also assume they can perform a few algebraic manipulations? ... No, not safely.

So. We will assume they can do the simple arithmetic operations, and add that to the prerequisites sheet. But now we will have to add something to our objectives, because they need to know about conversions and we can't assume they already know this. We will have to add this to the things we must teach.

Here is an example of what your list of prerequisites might look like.

Prerequisites: Television Repairman

1. The student must have the ability to use small machine and hand tools. Such tools include an electric drill, saw, pliers, hammer, and chisels.
2. The student must be able to read at the fifth-grade level.
3. The student must be able to work in environments of extreme cold and hot climates, from $-20°$ to $+98°$ Fahrenheit.
4. The student must be physically fit and cannot have physical handicaps of the type that would restrict the student from job duties. A student must be able to work on the roof of a house or apartment without getting dizzy.
5. Assume knowledge of basic arithmetic operations, including addition, subtraction, multiplication, and division.
6. Student must be interested in working outdoors.
7. Normal color vision is desirable, but not essential.
8. Assume that the student has, or can obtain, a valid driver's license.
9. Assume that the student's biases or prejudices are not so strong as to prevent him from interacting with a wide variety of customers.

7 Measuring Instruments

Prerequisites Test

If the design of your course is based on the documents you have developed so far, then it *matters* whether students can actually do the things you have assumed they can do. To find out, prepare a test based solely on the prerequisites. Develop items that answer the question, "what must the student do to convince me that he has the skills I have assumed he has?"

Administer this test to students as they enter the course. If very few or none of the students can perform according to one of your assumptions, and if such performance is necessary, you have only two choices. You can either send students away for remedial instruction before you allow them into the course, or you can decide to teach them the missing skill. When you decide on the second alternative, erase the skill from your prerequisites sheet and add it to your objectives.

When students come into a course lacking various prerequisite skills or knowledge, the normal response is to provide remedial instruction. But students *also* enter a course knowing *more* than the prerequisites assume. In this case, remedial action should be applied to the course itself so students will not be bored by being taught what they already know.

Criterion Examination (Post-test)

As the prerequisite test is constructed *solely* from the statement of prerequisites, the criterion exam, or "post-test," is constructed *solely* from the course objectives. The object is to determine how well the student's performance at the end of instruction coincides with performance called for in the objectives. The object is *not* to see how well the student retains whatever he happened to be told during the course. The difference is an important one.

It is possible to rank students at the end of a course according to how much they learned (a typical technique in an academic course). They can also be evaluated on the basis of how closely their performance approximates the performance called for in the course objectives. In this case, the concern is not with comparing students against *each other,* but with a comparison of each student against a predefined criterion. This orientation influences the way in which test items are constructed. It calls for the creation of test items that will determine whether or not the student can perform as required, rather than for test items that are "difficult" enough so there will always be some students who fail. For example: If one of the objectives of the course calls for the student to be able to change a tire with a certain set of tools within two minutes, then the appropriate test item is to ask him to change the tire with those tools within two minutes. If *all* students can perform as specified, it is wrong to make the test item more difficult arbitrarily. If *none* of the students can perform, one does not make the test item easier ... instead, the instruction is improved. After all, the object is to teach students, not fail them.

The following guidelines are offered for the preparation of the criterion examination:

1. Use the objectives as your guide. Prepare as many items as necessary to find out how well the student meets each objective. In some cases, only one item is appropriate, as in the tire-changing example above. In other cases, you may feel that several items are needed to make an assessment.

2. Create items that call for the same kind of behavior specified in the objective. If an objective calls for a student to
use a certain tool, then create test items that cause him to
use the tool. In such a case, it would not be appropriate
to ask him to write an essay about the use of the tool or
to answer multiple-choice questions about the use of the
tool. If an objective calls for an ability to repair something,
then the appropriate test item is one that asks the student
to repair. Again, multiple-choice items are not appropriate.
If an objective asks the student to be able to talk about
something rather than do it, then an oral item or essay
item is appropriate.

On the following pages are examples of objectives and test
items. Some are appropriate for testing the objective, and some
are *not* appropriate. Items that are *appropriate* for testing the
objectives are checked.

Objective

Using a slide rule, be able to find the log of a three-digit number.

Test Items

1. Describe in your own words how to find a logarithm on a slide rule.
2. Using a table of logarithms, find the log of:
   a. .00872
   b. 3.24
   c. 9716
√3. Using your slide rule, find the log of the following numbers:
   a. 456
   b. 0.0752
   c. 34.5
4. Identify the mantissa in each of the following:
   a. 0.602
   b. 1.398
   c. 2.659

Objective

Given a pair of earphones and a pure tone generator, be able to tell the
difference between two consecutive tones that are 50 cycles apart.

Test Items

✓1. Discriminate between two tones of 5000 and 5050 cycles.
2. Define the range of audible frequencies.
3. Explain in your own words the theory of audition.
4. List the steps in measuring a just-noticeable difference.

Objective

Given a wood lathe, appropriate tools, and rectangular walnut stock, be able to turn a table leg suitable for a coffee table. The leg should be tapered in any way desired by the student, provided the narrow end differs from the wide end by at least ½″ in diameter.

Test Items

✓1. Construct a table leg from rectangular walnut that contains at least a ½″ taper, using the lathe and tools provided.
2. Describe the wood lathe and related tools.
3. List, in proper sequence, the steps required to construct a set of table legs.
4. Describe the advantages of legs.

Objective

From three lists of merchandise and their prices, be able to fill out three appropriate sales slips without error.

Test Items

1. Describe in detail and in your own words the difference between the three types of sales slips.
2. Identify the three sales slips in terms of color and size, and determine the price range of merchandise recorded on each.
✓3. Fill out the three attached sales slips for each list of merchandise.
4. Supply the customer with a cash register receipt instead of completing the three forms.

Objective

Given a carburetor that is misadjusted but which contains no malfunctions, be able to readjust it for maximum performance within 5 minutes. Maximum performance is defined by the oscilloscope pattern specified by the instructor.

Test Items

1. Identify the correct pattern as seen on the oscilloscope from several examples illustrated in the carburetor manual.
2. Describe and define the functions of a carburetor.
√3. Reset the misadjusted carburetor so that the correct pattern will appear on the oscilloscope within five minutes.
4. List the difference between the two-barrel type versus the four-barrel type of carburetor.

Objective

Be able to assemble an M-16 rifle correctly, blindfolded, within ten minutes.

Test Items

1. List the parts of the M-16 rifle.
2. Describe the action of the M-16 rifle and why it is superior to others. Also state the history of the rifle and pertinent facts concerning its use.
3. Memorize the location of each part on the table so that a faster assembling time can be achieved.
√4. On the table in front of you is a disassembled M-16 rifle. Identify the parts with your fingers and assemble the rifle within ten minutes. Once assembled, check and inspect for accuracy.

Objective

Given scissors, comb, and brush, be able to shape and style a client's hair to her satisfaction, taking into consideration facial contour and hair color and texture, within a half hour. Acceptable performance is achieved when the client is satisfied.

Test Items

1. Explain in your own words the methods of good hair grooming.
√2. Given scissors, comb, and brush, style a client's hair, taking into consideration her facial contour and hair color and texture, within a half hour.
3. List ten types of hairstyles and indicate their current popularity.

8 Types of Performance

There may be several instructional procedures from which to choose when developing a lesson. There is, of course, the lecture. There are films, slides, filmstrips, mock-ups, books, manuals, demonstrations, discussions, recitation, practice, and more. Since all of these procedures are not equally effective all of the time, and since some of them are appropriate some of the time, the question is . . . how to decide when to use what?

Some teachers decide which procedures and materials to use on the basis of what they are most comfortable with; one may be most comfortable with the lecture, while another may feel more at ease with slides and discussion. Though it may be acceptable for amateurs to select their teaching procedures this way, the professional wants a more rational basis for making his decisions. After all, the professional instructor is an individual who can make his selections in a manner that results in efficient instruction. (We would be in a fine fix if the surgeon only performed those operations he is "comfortable" with, or if the carpenter refused to use any tool but the hammer because he "likes" the feel of it.)

Fortunately there is a sounder basis for choosing instructional procedures, and this chapter will discuss the first step.

In the way one selects a tool from the toolbox by knowing what he needs to accomplish, one chooses an instructional procedure by first identifying the kind of *performance* he wants to develop. As Briggs has pointed out, "The best available basis for the needed matching of media with objectives, is a rationale by which the kind of learning involved in each educational objective is stated in terms of the learning conditions required."*

There are several different kinds of performance, and different procedures and materials are appropriate for teaching each. For example: A simulator might be highly appropriate for teaching someone to fly a plane, but it would be inappropriate for teaching him how to spell. That much seems clear. But why is this so? It is because two kinds of performance are involved; one kind is facilitated or made easier by using a simulator, and the other isn't. Let's consider the types of performance.

Dr. Robert Gagné has presented an excellent and scholarly description of eight different kinds of performance, and has attempted to show which conditions are most appropriate for facilitating the learning of each of these performance types.** In an attempt to simplify the job of course preparation, we have modified Gagné's eight categories into only five: discrimination, problem-solving, recall, manipulation, and speech.

If you determine which of these five types of performance is the one *primarily associated with* each of your task steps, you will be in a good position to select course content, procedures, and materials. The expression "primarily associated with" is an important one to notice, because each task consists of several types of performance, and because each task step may involve two or more types. Performance types are interrelated. For example: Although the process of mixing cake batter involves manipulation, it also involves knowing what to do and knowing how to recognize when it has been done properly. The important thing is to identify the *principal* type of performance associated

*Leslie J. Briggs and others, *Instructional Media: A Procedure for the Design of Multi-media Instruction, a Critical Review of Research, and Suggestions for Future Research,* Palo Alto, Calif.: American Institutes for Research, 1965, p. 176.

**Robert M. Gagné, *The Conditions of Learning.* New York: Holt, Rinehart & Winston, Inc., 1965, p. 308. This book is highly recommended for those who wish to develop a course according to the most scientific techniques available.

with each step, to simplify the identification of course content. With the principal type of performance identified, content selection becomes a matter of answering the question, "What are the enabling skills needed to perform this step?" If, for example, a step calls for selection of the proper tool, what skills does the student need? Knowledge? An ability to discriminate bolt sizes? Manual skill? The answer identifies the instructional content associated with this step of the task. But selection of content and instructional procedures is facilitated to the degree principal performance type is identified for each step of each task.

Discrimination
(Knowing When To Do It, Knowing When It's Done)

Discrimination means being able to tell the difference between two or more things. When you hear the difference between a good note and a sour note, you are discriminating. You discriminate when you perceive that one object is red and another blue. Discrimination is involved in being able to taste the difference between two cups of coffee and in feeling the difference between rough surfaces and smooth surfaces.

Being able to tell whether two objects are alike or different is one form of discrimination. Another form of discrimination is being able to tell whether one thing is the same or different from a mental image of what it ought to be. How can you tell when you have a flat tire? You discriminate a difference between the lumpy driving you are experiencing and your mental image of smooth driving. How do you know when a particular task needs to be done? You discriminate that there is a difference between the situation or environment and your picture of what it ought to be like. How can you tell the difference between a good job and a bad job? You compare what has been done with your memory of what ought to be done.

Discrimination between two objects is taught by showing the student pairs of the things you want him to see a difference between. The difference between these pairs of objects is gradually reduced until the student is able to make discriminations fine enough to be satisfactory. For example: If it is necessary to teach the student to recognize pitch differences between pairs of tones, he would be played pairs of tones that are obviously different in pitch and then asked to tell whether the second is higher or lower than the first. The difference in pitch between the two tones would be gradually reduced until the student was able to discriminate at a suitable level.

The second kind of discrimination is taught by giving the student practice in comparing single items or situations with his knowledge of what they should be like. He is given practice in saying whether a thing is, or is not, consistent with his picture of it. Such practice increases the accuracy of his mental image and increases his ability to make proper discriminations. For example: If a student needed to learn how to recognize when a circle was "round enough," he would be shown a series of circles of varying degrees of roundness and asked to compare each one with his mental criterion. He would be given immediate knowledge of results so that he would know how to correct his mental image. He would also be shown pairs of circles, one unacceptable and one acceptable in each pair, and provided with any other information that would help him with the discrimination.

Wherever Task Detailing Sheets list a step that calls for the student to be able to distinguish one thing from another, to tell when a proper job has been done, to tell when a task needs to be done, or to see the difference between correct and incorrect, the principal type of performance called for is discrimination.

Problem-solving
(How To Decide What To Do)

Once you discriminate (perceive) that a job needs to be done, you normally proceed to do the job. Sometimes, however, you see that something needs to be done, but you don't know what to do. You see your TV picture rolling or tearing, so you know that something needs to be fixed. What to do? Find the trouble. You can't fix it if you can't find it. The process of finding the trouble is called problem-solving, and involves teaching the student procedures that will lead him to locate the trouble.

Whenever a task step calls for the student to figure out the best way of doing something or to decide what to do next, he is being asked to engage in problem-solving. Problem-solving is taught by showing the student those cues or symptoms that should lead him to conclude that problem-solving is called for, by showing him relationships between these symptoms and possible causes, and by giving him practice on the actual thing or situation needing remedial action. It is done by showing him symptoms and letting him find his way to the trouble. It is NOT done by showing him a trouble and asking him to guess what symptoms would appear. Thus, problem-solving on TV sets is taught better on the set itself than through lectures. It is taught best by having the student *solve* as many problems as possible, not having him talk about it, write about it, or answer multiple-choice questions about it.

Recall
(Knowing What To Do, Knowing Why To Do It)

If you decided that the dinner table needed to be set, you would immediately know which plates and silverware were needed. If you saw that a roast needed carving, you would know that a carving knife was the thing to get and use. These things that you know are things you can recall. Whenever you say that there are some things the student just "has to know," you are asking for performance based on recall. When the student is expected to shout out the tools and parts he will need when you say "carburetor adjustment," one is asking for performance based on recall.

There is a special class of recall called sequencing, or chaining. Sometimes it is essential that a very precise sequence of steps be followed in performing a task. Learning those steps in order is an example of chaining. For example: There is a very precise order of steps that must be followed in performing surgical operations. It is important that those who do this task know which step follows every other step.

Although the process of recall is an internal, invisible one, it is still the principal performance associated with a great deal of visible activity. For example: If you recite the names of all the states, the principal feature of the performance is that of recall rather than that of speaking. If, however, you are trying to learn to speak a given sentence with a particular accent, then speaking is the principal feature of this performance rather than recall. Whenever the principal feature of a task step is that it requires knowing *what* to do more than *how* to do it, the principal type of performance is recall.

The techniques used to teach recall depend on the nature of the performance desired. If a student is to make a certain response whenever he *hears* a certain sound, the technique indicated is one that presents the sound and makes the student respond until he can do it without help. If the student is expected to be able to do something whenever he *sees* a certain thing, then a visual technique that shows him the object or cue and allows him to practice the response is used. If the recall is related to knowing how something works, then a demonstration-lecture is appropriate, if followed by practice wherein the student is asked to describe (orally or in writing) the relationships that go to make up the substance of "how the thing works."

Once the problem has been identified, the skilled worker, the person who has learned just which tools and materials are required to solve the problem, is able to use the tools and materials in the proper sequence of steps in performing the task. The highly skilled worker requires a minimum of memory aids to help him remember what to do and when, though such aids might be used whenever they can simplify either the job or the training. Knowing what to do, what to use, and the order or sequence in which to perform a task, are examples of the mental performance known as recall.

While the actual process of recalling or remembering is a mental or internal kind of performance, it is quite possible to tell whether this kind of performance is going on. This is essentially the kind of information obtained through paper-and-pencil tests. If a girl, for example, is able to answer correctly when you ask her which sewing machine attachment is needed in order to sew a hem, you know she has performed a correct recall; you know she has the correct knowledge.

The two principal ways in which we interact with our environment are through the things we do and the things we say,

and visible performance always appears in the form of either
moving or speaking. But this does not mean that a great deal
of knowledge or recall may not be required in order to perform
the doing or speaking. Where knowing *what* to do is much
more important than knowing *how* to do it (because the doing
involves a universal skill, as in pushing buttons), recall is listed
as the principal type of performance.

Manipulation
(How To Do It)

Knowing *what* to do isn't always the same as knowing *how*
to do it. For example: If you knew that the next step in a task
was to go and get a certain tool, you could also perform the step
... because you know how to walk and know where the tool is
located. In this case, knowing what to do *is* the same as knowing
how to do it. But you may know that in order to take out an
appendix, it is necessary to make an incision with a scalpel. That
doesn't mean you know how to do it or where to do it. We
realize that this may seem like a trivial point, but it is worth
making, because instructors sometimes fail to follow theory with
practice. Sometimes they behave as though they believe that if
the student knows *what* to do, he also knows *how* to do it. As a
result, they do a good job of teaching students how to *talk* about
doing something, but fail to teach him to actually *do* it. It is
important, therefore, to identify the various kinds of manipulative skills required of the student. But if you find yourself
listing *only* manipulation on your Task Detailing Sheets, something is wrong. Either task steps are not accurately listed, or your
decisions about which performance types are *principally* involved need review. Manipulation is taught by providing an
opportunity to manipulate under conditions as close as possible
to those found on the job.

Through recall, the student will know what to do when using
tools, for example, but actual practice with the tools is the best
way to teach him how to use them. We could *tell* you how to
ride a unicycle, or we could *show* you how it is done by film or
by demonstration. Neither of these procedures would be successful in teaching you to actually *do* it. We could teach you how to
talk about riding a unicycle, or we could teach you how to write

essays about it and even how to write songs about it. Again, none of these procedures is likely to result in your actually being able to ride it.

Speech
(How To Say It)

For many jobs, speech is merely a form of communicating knowledge. Some tasks, however, require that speech be used in a particular way; for some tasks, speech is an essential feature of desired performance. This is true in the case of the announcer, the actor, the salesman, and the telephone operator. In these instances, the way in which the speaking is done is essential to job success, so appropriate objectives must be prepared and relevant instruction included in the course. When the style of verbal behavior called for in a task step is important to job success, the principal characteristic of the performance is speaking rather than knowing or recalling. It matters, for example, whether a waitress communicates with a customer through a pleasant tone of voice or a cranky one, even though the content of her speaking is based on recall.

The principal technique for teaching specific speech characteristics is one involving imitation, practice, and immediate knowledge of results. The tape recorder is an indispensable tool. It not only allows the student to hear a model as frequently as necessary, but enables him to hear his own efforts immediately after making them. When, as is very often the case, facial expression and gestures are also related to speech style, the video tape recorder is hard to beat. In the absence of this device, a mirror is the next best thing.

Now, if you will fill in the principal type of performance called for in each step listed on your Task Detailing Sheets, you will have completed an important step in the selection of appropriate instructional procedures. One comment. If you find you do not like the words we have used in describing performance categories, describe them in a way that makes sense to yourself. Use whatever words you please, but don't slip by the step of identifying performance. If you do, you will find yourself selecting instructional procedures and materials more on the basis of superstition and guesswork than rational decision-making.

9 Selection of Instructional Procedures

There are many techniques for presenting information and for transmitting skills; since not all are equally effective in reaching each instructional goal, it will be useful to discuss the bases on which intelligent choices can be made. A word of caution, however, is in order. Though schools and instructors have been in existence for centuries, and though educational researchers have been at work for decades, we do not yet have a science-based guide that tells us how to make accurate selection of appropriate instructional strategy. Psychological research has provided some insight into this problem, and in this chapter we will try to translate that information into usable guides in the selection of instructional procedures and materials.

Characteristics of Instructional Procedures and Materials

The instructional procedures and materials toolbox is a full one. It ranges from apprenticeship training, simulators, self-instructional demonstrations, and field trips, through motion pictures, television, filmstrips, transparencies, disk and tape recordings, to the graphic media of charts, graphs, diagrams, maps, cartoons, and the symbolic media of the written and spoken word.

Each instructional medium has specific characteristics, or features. For example: Lecturing is easy to do and is, therefore, convenient for the instructor; but it forces the student to be relatively passive. One feature of the magnetic tape or disk recording is the organized simulation of a series of sounds. If listening discrimination is essential to the learning objective, the audio playback device is likely to have features most relevant to achievement of efficient learning.

Projection devices also have distinct features. Slides, transparencies, filmstrips, motion pictures, and television have the common characteristic of presenting a photographic reproduction of reality. . . a mirror image of life, so to speak. Magnification is another common feature, as is color. Editing possibility is a feature of the slide and the transparency, making possible timely changes and updating of content. The filmstrip, in contrast, features a fixed order of presentation. Adding a tape or disk recording to these picture devices adds a sound-message capability.

With time-lapse and slow- and fast-motion photography, the motion picture can expand and compress the real time scale. Animation, X-ray, and micro-photography can reveal processes and concepts invisible to the eye. A documentary record of an important event may be easily reproduced, history may be re-created, and on-site visits made anywhere in the world via the film.

One feature common to several instructional techniques is direct student participation. Supervised on-the-job training, for example, is an instructional procedure that has long been used by vocational-technical educators when development of manipulative skill is the primary goal. Simulators also allow skill development, as do some mock-ups and working models.

Much has been written about the characteristics or features of the many instructional techniques and devices currently available. More complete information and guidance on the characteristics and capabilities of these materials are provided in Chapter 14.

Advantages of Instructional Procedures and Materals

There is a large difference, however, between a feature or characteristic and an advantage. A feature or characteristic only becomes an advantage if it is appropriate or relevant to reaching some goal. For example: One of the features of a pair of roller skates is that they are relatively inexpensive. But is this feature an advantage? An advantage for what? If the goal is to get to South America by the fastest means available, the fact that roller skates are inexpensive is no advantage at all.

We have in our toolbox a small screwdriver with a blade small enough to fit tiny screws. Is this feature an advantage? It depends entirely on what we are trying to accomplish... it depends on our objective. If our immediate goal is to turn a large screw, then the small blade *feature* is clearly *not* an *advantage*. One feature of a small car is that it can be parked more easily than a large station wagon. Is this an advantage? It is if your goal is to do a lot of city driving. But if the goal is to carry as many bushels of apples as possible in one trip to the market, then the characteristic of "smallness" is not an advantage.

Selecting Appropriate Procedures

Hopefully, the point has been made that the selection of appropriate teaching procedures begins with determining precisely what the performance objectives are. With the type of performance identified for each part of each task, it is possible to go on to identifying the general class of procedure, or combination of procedures, appropriate for reaching *each* objective. For example: If one objective is, "Given two pairs of engine sounds, the student must be able to *identify* the one most representative of a smooth-running engine," then some form of *audio* instruction is appropriate. If one step in learning to perform a task is learning to *recognize* when a table has been properly set, then some form of *visual* technique is appropriate; a drawing, or slide, or photograph, or film might be used. A tape recording or a lecture would be less appropriate in reaching the objective.

If one of the objectives calls for the student to be able to actually *set* a table, then a different technique is called for. First, he should be taught to discriminate between a properly set and improperly set table; then he should be given actual practice. For this objective, a table and utensils are more appropriate than a discussion or a filmstrip.

Here are three guides to follow in the accomplishment of the second step in instructional procedures selection, the identification of procedures related to each of the performance objectives.

1. Choose the technique that most closely approximates the performance conditions called for by the objective. If the objective calls for the student to do something in response to what he *sees,* select a technique that most closely approximates the seeing to which he is to respond. For example: If the machinist needs to be able to tell the difference between metals by looking at them, provide the student with something to look at. Actual samples would be better than pictures; colored pictures would be better than black and white; any kind of picture or visual representation would be better than instruction by radio. If the student will be expected to tell the difference between materials by feeling them, just telling him how to tell the difference isn't as good as guided practice, where guided practice is defined as "actual doing by the student accompanied by verbal instruction by the instructor."

2. Choose the technique that causes the student to perform in a manner most closely approximating the performance called for on the job. If, in response to a visual cue or stimulus, the student will be expected to say something, select the technique that will give him practice in saying. If, in response to an auditory situation, the student will be expected to repair something, then select a technique that will give him practice in repairing. If an objective calls for a student to be able to describe relationships between parts of a system, select the technique that will cause him to do this; in this instance, some form of recitation technique would be better than the showing of a film.

3. Choose the technique that will allow the student to make the largest number of relevant responses per unit time. For example: Suppose the welder has to learn to recognize when his torch flame is properly adjusted to perform a particular task. If a photograph, slide, or film can show all the cues by which the student will be expected to discriminate proper flames from improper flames, these techniques would be better than the actual flame itself. Why? Because with a notebook or photographs or a tray of slides you can give the student much more discrimination practice in fifteen minutes than you could if you actually had to adjust a flame to show each of the good and bad features you want him to practice with. Although slides or photographs would be appropriate for reaching the discrimination objective, they are not appropriate for reaching the performance objective. There, it is better to provide actual flame-adjusting practice. Since practice isn't much good until the student can tell when he is doing it right and when he is doing it wrong, discrimination training would come first and actual practice second. The discrimination part would be taught faster with slides or pictures, but practice should be accomplished on the best available approximation of the actual device, and as soon after the discrimination phase as possible. Here is another example. The objective is to teach prospective woodshop instructors and on-the-job supervisors to discriminate by sound cues the various problems that arise when beginners operate the single surface planer. When properly fed, this machine gives off a "normal" hum, and any variation from this sound indicates trouble or inefficient utilization. Too heavy a bite in cutting the wood lowers the sound pitch; too light a bite produces a vibrating sound. If the wood is fed so the grain is in the wrong direction, a chipping sound is heard; if imperfect wood is inserted, other audible clues can be detected. The objective would be reached better by a demonstration incorporating a programmed tape recording of the sound discriminations to be mastered than by a lecture about sounds or by a filmstrip showing the improper way wood can be fed into the planer.

After those procedures and materials most relevant to desired performance have been identified, the next step is to select among them on the basis of administrative criteria. The most appropriate technique isn't always an available technique; the most appropriate technique isn't always practical or within the budget. For example: The best way to teach an astronaut how to work under weightless conditions is to give him practice under zero gravity. Since this would be impractical and very costly, a substitute must be found: a variety of simulators have been constructed for this purpose.

If it is determined that slides, filmstrips, and photographs would work equally well, select the one that is most available and most likely to be used. If slide or filmstrip projectors are available but normally located somewhere other than the class-room, photographs would be preferable.

Let's try the guides on one or two examples. Suppose an objective calls for the student to be able to respond, in French, to spoken questions in French. Applying Guide 1, we see that among the appropriate techniques are those that can speak French to the student; in other words, audio techniques. This might be done by the instructor, or by a record, by audio tape, by television, or by film. Applying Guide 2, we find that the student could make an appropriate response to any of these techniques, so none are eliminated on this basis. In applying Guide 3, however, we are likely to rule out at least the instructor for logistic reasons. It is likely that each student will get less practice if the instructor is forced to provide the verbal stimulus than if each student were provided with his own tape recorder or language laboratory station. A film is likely to be eliminated for similar reasons. Then, in comparing what is appropriate with what is available and practical, the language laboratory might have to be eliminated if one does not exist in the training situation and if the budget is not likely to provide one in the fore-seeable future. If tape playback equipment is equally unavailable, the instructor himself may be the best practical alternative.

Here's another example. One of the skills involved in driving a car is the ability to sense (discriminate) potential dangers. Such dangers are detected by the eye and by the ear. Applying Guide 1, we find that appropriate techniques for presenting relevant cues or stimuli would be through actual driving, through sound films, or through slides or pictures accompanied by audio tape. Applying Guide 2, we find that the appropriate response can be made to any of these techniques, since it is an identification response that is wanted. (This would not be the case for the objective requiring the student to learn what to do in response to danger detection.) Applying Guide 3, we would rule out the actual driving situation, because far more discrimination practice can be systematically given through films or slides than through actual driving. We would rule out the actual driving situation when administrative criteria are applied, because it would be considerably less economical and less practical than the use of the specially designed films already available. So, in this case (detecting dangers) a film would be most appropriate, followed in appropriateness by video tape, slides, and the actual driving situation.

The strategy is to pick those techniques most relevant to the type of performance involved and *then* make final selections on the basis of availability and probable use.

To summarize, selection of instructional procedures involves:

1. Identifying the type of performance desired,
2. Identifying those procedures most relevant to the desired performance, and
3. Selecting those that are most practical from among those that are appropriate.

To help you identify procedures and materials that might be useful in teaching your own vocation or profession, some available types and sources are listed in Chapter 14. You might also find it useful to write to your own professional society for a list of instructional materials relating to your field. Most societies have prepared such summaries.

10 Sequencing Instructional Units

Special consideration must be given to the sequence in which the instructional units will be presented, because it is known that what is meaningful for the instructor is not necessarily meaningful for the student. Units should be sequenced in an order that is most meaningful to the student. For example: If you suddenly had to learn how to repair a missile system, would you first want to be taught electronic theory, or would you first want to know what the system does and how to operate it? Do you think you could learn to understand the details of automobile repair if you didn't know what a car was? If you had to withdraw from a course for some reason, wouldn't you rather leave with a usable skill than merely with the theory and background leading to a skill?

Here are six guides to effective sequencing of instructional material.

1. *From general to specific.* Students mean something different than instructors when they agree they would like instruction to proceed from the "simple to the complex."

Whereas instructors tend to be comfortable with sequencing from the elements of a subject toward the big picture,
students generally find it more meaningful to move from
the big picture toward the details. Once the student knows
the subject matter, he can also find a specific-to-general
sequence meaningful. To apply this rule, you would begin
by teaching the student how to operate a machine before
you teach him how to repair it or before you teach him
any theory. Teach him *how* something works first, and
why it works that way later.

2. *Interest sequencing.* To maintain the motivation of the
student, start with a unit that contains information in
which he is highly interested at the beginning of the
course. For example: Since most students entering a locksmithing course seem to be highly interested in learning
how to pick a lock, the first lesson might teach them how
to pick *one kind* of lock. Identify those units that are most -
interesting to students, and then seed these units among
the others wherever possible.

3. *Logical sequencing.* Sometimes the subject matter dictates
that one unit be taught before another. For example: A
skin diver must be taught how to operate his breathing
equipment before he can be taught to perform underwater
maneuvers. Where it *is* necessary to teach one thing before
another, do so. But be careful! There isn't nearly as much
reason for this kind of sequencing as instructors like to
believe. A man doesn't have to know anything about
mathematics before he can be taught to repair a television
set; he doesn't have to know the theory of how an automobile engine works before he can learn how to adjust
a carburetor; and he doesn't have to know how to lay a
foundation before he can be taught to construct a roof.

4. *Skill sequencing.* If a man has to leave a course before
finishing it (for whatever reason), it is better to send him
away with the ability to do a complete, if lesser, job than
to send him away able only to talk about a job. For example: Teach a man everything he needs to know to become
a qualified plumber's helper first; then teach him what he

needs in addition to become a qualified plumber. Teach a man everything he needs to know about radio repair first, and then add what else he needs to know to become a television repairman.

5. *Frequency sequencing.* Which skills will a man use most frequently on the job? Teach him first those skills he will use most often; then sequence the rest of your units in order of decreasing usefulness or importance. This way, although you may fail to teach him one or two things because you run out of time, the skills he will be without will be those he will need least often. For example: Teach a locksmithing student how to make keys before you teach him how to change combinations; teach an automobile repairman how to adjust a carburetor before you teach him how to weld an engine block; and teach a television repairman how to change a tube before you teach him how to change a resistor.

6. *Total job practice.* Some courses systematically give a student knowledge and practice in each element of a job, but allow the course to end without ever giving the student an opportunity to practice the entire job. The student needs a chance to practice the entire job as much as he needs practice in the bits and pieces of the job. At least five per cent of course time should be devoted to such practice, during which the student actually practices performing the total job under conditions as similar as possible to those he will face when the course is over.

11 Lesson Plan Development

The lesson plan is the instructional prescription, the blueprint that describes the activities the student may engage in to reach the objectives of the course. It is an administrative document that describes how facilities, time, instructor, and content will be organized so that the largest number of students will develop the highest degree of skill. As several sources of information are used in the derivation of objectives, several sources are used as a basis for outlining instructional activities: objectives, the description of prerequisites, the Task Detailing Sheets, and all information about materials, facilities, and time constraints.

The essence of lesson planning is to develop instructional units that are maximally meaningful to the student and maximally effective in the use of time, space, and personnel.

It is during development of the lesson plan that it becomes necessary to make concessions to the rules and procedures of your institution ... to force a few round pegs into square holes, so to speak. If the institution has fixed rules about the length of class periods and about what students must do during class hours—that is, if the institution is designed more for the convenience of administrators than students—it will be necessary to make more radical modifications than is the case when an institution is more flexible. But there will be restrictions or constraints of one sort or another even in the most flexible of institutions, and this is the place to compromise between the ideal and the possible.

There are probably as many different lesson plan formats as there are instructors, and there is nothing particularly magical about the format we are suggesting (Figure 7) ... with one exception: it specifically calls for identifying what the *student* will be doing during each phase of instruction, thus providing a good check on the appropriateness of the selections of instructional procedures and materials. The form is one which, if followed, makes it impossible to fall into the trap of developing a course principally on the basis of what an instructor wants to do rather than on the basis of what students need to do in order to achieve.

There are seven general steps, or activities, in the development of lesson plans. These steps consist of outlining the learning units, identifying the type of performance involved, identifying appropriate content, rough sequencing the units, selecting instructional procedures and materials, final sequencing, and completion of lesson plan details.

1. The first step is to outline roughly the meaningful units of instruction. Each item of this outline is an answer to the question, "What do I have to do, and what does the student have to do, in order for him to achieve objective X or to perform task Y?" To keep the instruction as meaningful as possible to the student, and to enable him to leave each instructional session with a recognizable skill he didn't have at its beginning, instructional sessions are organized on the basis of tasks and objectives rather than on the basis of content. The rough outline of instructional units is based on the Task Detailing Sheets and the objectives.

2. The second step is to identify the type of student performance associated with each step of the tasks to be learned. This performance has already been identified on the Task Detailing Sheets and will be used as the primary basis for the selection of instructional procedures.

3. The tasks and objectives to be taught are next put into a preliminary sequence, following the recommendations presented in Chapter 10.

LESSON PLAN

Lesson Unit Objective: _____

Procedure	Student Activity	Estimated Time

Figure 7.

4. Content is then identified on the basis of the tasks to be taught. Content is selected in answer to the question, "What does the student need to know to achieve this objective or to perform this task?" If time remains after the course is structured on the basis of knowledge and skills required for satisfactory performance, additional content of the "nice to know" variety may be added. First priority, however, is for that content that will assist the student to become most useful in the least amount of time.

5. Instructional procedures appropriate to the kind of performance to be developed at each stage are then identified, and available materials and devices are listed. Selection among these is made, based on the recommendations contained in Chapter 9.

6. Sequencing of the units is reviewed and modified as required. Here the sequencing is adjusted to prevent students from having to sit in one place for long periods of time, and to provide variety through variation of instructional procedure.

7. Lesson plans are then completed. Adjustments are made to insure continuity from one lesson to the next, to insure that the student is always informed of where he is and how far he has come, to insure that the student spends as much time as possible engaged in activities directly relevant to the objectives of the course, and to insure that the procedures selected can actually be implemented with the time and facilities available.

The lesson plan should be thought of as a guide to the way students and instructor will spend the day, rather than as a document that precisely dictates what must happen during each instructional minute. It is impossible to make perfect predictions about the exact amount of time required to reach each objective; as a result, instructional planning should contain a great deal of flexibility. Skilled graduates are produced by carefully specifying the objectives of instruction rather than by carefully specifying the procedures that must be followed throughout the instructional day. In a sense, it is reasonable to consider the objectives as the fail-safe mechanism that will guarantee your success, that will insure the development of students who can perform as expected. With clearly stated objectives in the hands of the instructor and in the hands of students, it is both safe and efficient to give students considerable freedom in the selection of procedures and activities they feel will be most useful in helping them achieve those objectives.

During the development of a course an instructor comes across many problems and questions that are difficult to answer. He is faced with many decisions about what to include and what to exclude, about extent of coverage and emphasis, about what the student can already do, and about what interests him. We would strongly urge you to consider the student as your ally, because in most cases he will be able to provide you with the answers to your questions. If you want to know whether an explanation is clear or meaningful, ask a student. If you want to know whether a particular technique succeeds in teaching, try it out on a student. After all, your job is to facilitate student behavior, and the very best way to find out how well you are doing is to ask the student.

On page 67 is an example of what a lesson plan sheet might look like when completed. Notice that the lesson is not organized to fit a fifty-minute hour. Rather, this example assumes the possibility of flexible scheduling, since it is much more efficient to control instruction by objectives than by arbitrary time blocks.

LESSON PLAN

Lesson Unit Objective: <u>To be able to take temperatures and read</u>
<u>thermometer scales</u>

Procedure	Student Activity	Estimated Time
Practice problem on scale reading.	Reading ther-mometer scales.	30 minutes

Demonstration of complete task.
  1. Sterilization.
  2. Preparation.
  3. Placement in mouth.
	Watching and asking questions.	20 minutes

Break.		10 minutes
Pair students off for guided practice. Assist students as required.	Practicing the task.	30 minutes
Break.		10 minutes
Individual performance test.	Each student takes instruc-tor's tempera-ture.	5 minutes per student

12 Improving Course Efficiency

No matter how scientific or systematic a procedure may be available through which to develop a course of instruction, the number of compromises that must be made with circumstances and local conditions makes it inevitable that the original course can still be improved. The fact that we still have a lot to learn about instructional design makes it certain that continued effort will result in further course improvement. Although the procedure we have outlined in this thin volume is based both on learning research results and on practical tryout in the classroom, there are many questions yet to be answered.

Fortunately the technique we have outlined contains within it procedures for checking the efficiency of a course and for spotting places where improvements can be made.

One of these procedures tells us how well the course succeeds in teaching what we have decided to teach; the other tells us how well we decided what to teach. The first involves checking student performance against the objectives, and the second involves checking the objectives against the job. These two procedures must be kept separate to avoid making the mistake of changing an objective because it wasn't reached rather than because it is irrelevant or outdated. A man could fail to perform a job adequately because he picked the wrong tool or because he picked the right tool but couldn't use it properly. The same is true of a course. A course could fail to produce students who are effectively prepared for a vocation because they were taught the wrong things or because they were taught the right things... but weren't taught them well enough.

Let us consider the first of these procedures ... checking course efficiency. The procedure is simple in theory, and only a little more difficult in practice. It consists of answering the question, "How well did students achieve *each* of the objectives I specified?" How well did student performance compare with the performance called for in the objectives?

The proper comparison is made between *final* performance of the student and the *terminal* (end-of-course) objectives, and the comparison is made one objective at a time. To determine how well your objectives were reached, you are *not* interested in how many objectives were reached *on the average;* rather, the interest is in the percentage of students that reached each objective. For example: If we were to say that eighty per cent of our students reached our objectives, you wouldn't have any information on the basis of which to improve our course. You couldn't tell from that kind of statistic *which* objectives were reached and which were not. Such a figure could mean any number of things. It could mean that eight out of ten students reached each of the objectives, or it could mean that *all* students reached eighty per cent of them and that all students failed to achieve twenty per cent of them.

What is wanted is a separate indicator for each objective. If, for example, an objective calls for students to be able to make a particular adjustment in five minutes or less, and if all students reach at least that level of skill, then the objective has been reached perfectly. You may discover later that the five-minute limit needs to be changed, but that is another matter. What is important is to determine how well you succeeded in doing what you set out to do.

If only seventy per cent of the students reached the required performance level, then thirty per cent of them *failed* to reach that level, regardless of how well they performed in other areas. In this case, you would have to consider yourself only seventy per cent successful in developing the level of performance you wanted. (There may be reasons beyond your control why the remaining thirty per cent can't perform, but the fact still remains that you failed to get them to the desired goal.)

What if these students could perform the adjustment in five minutes and *one* second? Sorry, but that's your problem. If *you* specified five minutes as the limit, then these students failed to perform to your standards. If five minutes and one second is as good as five minutes, by all means, adjust the objective—but not before checking to see how well you reached the goal as originally stated.

The information gained from this analysis will show you where course emphasis needs to be changed and where more effort would be warranted in course design. Further, it will allow you to make better decisions when faced with information about an inadequacy students may appear to have on the job, because you will be able to tell whether the inadequacy is the result of ineffective training or improperly selected objectives.

13 Improving Course Effectiveness

The course is *efficient* to the degree it does what it sets out to do. It is *effective* to the degree it sets out to do those things most related to the job or vocation to be taught. As we have seen, efficiency is checked by comparing actual student performance with the objectives. Effectiveness, on the other hand, is checked by comparing the objectives with the actual job or vocation. The effective vocational course is one that selects the appropriate objectives ... and causes each student to reach them.

There is good reason to keep checking on the appropriateness of objectives. Jobs change, and sometimes they change rapidly. Computer programming, for example, is a course that needs revision almost monthly if it is to keep up with the world. New tools become available, new techniques are introduced, new information must be mastered, and new environments appear. The vocational educator, probably more than anyone else, is painfully aware of the ways in which jobs change. And for just this reason, he needs to make periodic checks on the relevance of his course objectives.

The procedures for comparing objectives with job are more time consuming than difficult . . . but important. Here again, the student is the principal source of information. Here are five suggestions about how to check on the appropriateness of course objectives, presented in order of increasing difficulty. Unfortunately, the easiest ones are the least informative, but we are more interested in providing you with practical information than with tasks you are too busy to carry out.

1. Between one and two months after a student has left your course and reported for a job, call him on the telephone. By this time, he will have run into most of the problems, if any, that will develop because of any weaknesses in his training. Ask him to tell you what sort of things he is doing and how often he does them. Ask him what problems he has run into and why. Ask him what he can do particularly well. In other words, perform a task analysis over the telephone. But ask him about the *job,* not about the course. You already know how well he reached each of the course objectives. What you are looking for is information about how well the objectives match the job. If he volunteers information about the course, accept it without comment and then ask him more questions about what he actually does and about how well he is able to perform. How many students should you call (assuming that phone calls are within reason)? Keep calling until the answers begin to fall into a pattern, until the answers begin to become repetitious. Then stop and decide how your course objectives should be modified on the basis of what you have learned.

2. If calling a few students is impractical, send them a questionnaire asking about job conditions, the frequency with which they are asked to perform various tasks, what they could do well when they began the job, and where they are weak. In other words, ask the questions that will help you check on your course objectives. Although it may make the student feel better if you ask him how the course might be improved, put less weight on his answer than on his answers to questions about the job itself. While you may

be interested in what people say about course improvement, your course decisions should be based on more objective information . . . such as is obtained by comparing what the job *is* with your objectives . . . and as obtained by comparing your objectives with actual student performance.

3. Between one and two months after a student has reported for a job, visit him at his place of work. For some instructors, this is the simplest thing to do . . . for others it is impossible. If you can make such a visit, do the same thing suggested in the paragraph above. Ask about the *job,* not about the course. In addition, look around to see what machines and instruments are used and how they are maintained. Check to see what tools are in use and ask about new procedures.

4. Between one and two months after a man has reported for a job, talk to his supervisor. Talk with him on the telephone or visit him. Ask him how well your former student could perform the job when he first arrived and how well he can perform it now. Ask him what he could do particularly well, and ask him what his weaknesses are. But try to keep him talking about the job. Almost anyone who has ever been to school considers himself an expert in education, and almost everyone will be happy to tell you how you can improve your course. Listen politely, but not too intently. *You* are the expert instructor, and *you* will decide how the course can be improved. The supervisor doesn't know in detail what the course objectives are, and he is therefore in no position to compare student performance with the objectives. He *is* in a position to tell you how well a man is performing his work, and that is the information you need to help you make decisions about alterations in objectives. *This point is too important not to repeat.* You will not be able to prevent people from telling you how to teach and about how things were when *they* went to school, so the strategy to adopt is that of listening politely *without arguing.* When it is your turn to talk, ask another question about how well your former student performs.

5. If you are an instructor in a vocational school, get a summer job working at your vocation, if possible. If your employment situation allows it, this is an effective way of keeping up with your profession—even if you only manage a working summer every four or five years. If you happen to be a trainer in a corporation, however, this advice will be about as useful as a rubber key, because your summer will already be accounted for.

There are other activities that will help you keep up with what is new in your specialty... reading journals and trade papers and talking with people you know who are working experts in your field. But these are things you do anyhow and need not be elaborated on here.

If you act to make your course objectives correspond with the needs of the vocation, and if you act to cause each qualified student to reach these objectives, you can be sure of having a highly effective course... and you will be able to demonstrate your success as a professional instructor.

14 Sources of Instructional Materials

This chapter contains information about some specific types of procedures, materials, and devices that are currently available to the instructor. Four relevant and available textbooks have been keyed to topics of interest so that you can easily locate the pages containing the information you are seeking.

In addition, a variety of references has been provided. These references include selected instructional information, information on programmed instruction, sources of vocational-technical instructional materials, and a list of relevant periodicals and journals.

Textbooks on the Selection, Utilization, and Preparation of Instructional Materials*

	Brown	DeKieffer	Erickson	Wittich
Television	210-245, 361-362	64-65	77-80, 114-115, 215-224, 253-259	407-429
Radio	201-209	60-63	72-73	271-276
Sound recordings	194-201, 208-209, 348-360, 362-368, 525-535	56-60	188-189, 197-206, 241-246, 286-288, 339-346	265-309
Graphics production	369-386, 464-494, 503-504	9-27	282-316	108-148
Display materials	267-295	11-27, 30-32	248, 283-286	149-171, 230-231
3-D materials (models, mock-ups, realia)	297-313, 413-436	14-17, 23-25	44-47, 120-124, 233-235	208-237
Demonstrations	315-327	19-27	155, 217, 233-235	
Dramatizations	328-338, 347	29-30	6, 25, 45	301-302
Discussions & Lectures	338-347	64	125-126, 215-224	

Community resources (field trips, museums)	387-412		231-233	249-264
Projected still pictures	142-162, 437-463, 476-477, 535-544	33-51	58-70, 325-339	311-352
Motion pictures	163-187, 494-504, 535-538, 545-555	33-51, 81-83	144-182, 275-281, 346-359	353-406
Programmed instruction & teaching machines	247-264		80-86, 182-196, 259-264	467-493
Multi-media presentations	154, 465	51-54	182-196, 264-266	430-462
Facilities & classroom design	505-521	67-75	109-120	284-285, 418, 478
Sources of materials, supplies, instruments	571-584		363-370	477-494

*This guide to information on specific procedures, materials, and devices is keyed by page numbers to the following books:

Brown, J. W.; Lewis, R. B.; and Harcleroad, F. F. *A-V Instruction: Materials and Methods* (2nd ed.). New York: McGraw-Hill Book Co., Inc., 1964, 592 pages.
DeKieffer, R. E. *Audiovisual Instruction*. New York: The Center for Applied Research in Education, 1965, 117 pages.
Erickson, C. W. H. *Fundamentals of Teaching with Audiovisual Technology*. New York: The Macmillan Co, 1965, 384 pages.
Wittich, W. A., and Schuller, C. F. *Audiovisual Materials: Their Nature and Use* (3rd ed.). New York: Harper & Row, Publishers, 1962, 500 pages.

Instructional Techniques
and Procedures

BLOOM, B. S. (ed.); ENGELHART, M. D.; FURST, E. J.; HILL, W. H.; and KRATHWOHL, D. R. *Taxonomy of Educational Objectives. Handbook I: Cognitive Domain*. New York: David McKay, Inc., 1956.

BRIGGS, L. J.; CAMPEAU, P. L.; GAGNÉ, R. M.; and MAY, M. A. *Instructional Media: A Procedure for the Design of Multi-media Instruction, a Critical Review of Research, and Suggestions for Future Research.* Palo Alto, Calif.: American Institutes for Research, 1963.

COX, R. C. "Item Selection Techniques and Evaluation of Instructional Objectives," *Bulletin,* Learning Research and Development Center, Univ. of Pittsburgh, Vol. 2, No. 2 (Dec., 1965).

GAGNÉ, R. M. *The Conditions of Learning.* New York: Holt, Rinehart & Winston, Inc., 1965.

GLASER, R. "The Design of Instruction," *Bulletin,* Learning Research and Development Center, Univ. of Pittsburgh (1966).

————."Toward a Behavioral Science Base for Instructional Design," *Bulletin,* Learning Research and Development Center, Univ. of Pittsburgh, pp. 771-806.

HARLESS, J. H., "The Ugly Duckling Learns To Fly," *NSPI Journal,* Vol. 5 (1966), pp. 3-6.

JACOBS, P. I.; MAIER, M. H.; and STOLUROW, L. W. *A Guide to Evaluating Self-instructional Programs.* New York: Holt, Rinehart & Winston, Inc., 1966.

KRATHWOHL, D. R.; BLOOM, B. S.; and MASIA, B. B. *Taxonomy of Educational Objectives. Handbook II: Affective Domain.* New York: David McKay, Inc., 1964.

MCGEHEE, W., and THAYER, P. W. *Training in Business and Industry.* New York: John Wiley & Sons, Inc., 1964.

MCKEACHIE, W. J., with KIMBLE, G. *Teaching Tips.* Ann Arbor, Mich.: The George Wahr Publishing Co., 1965.

MAGER, R. F. *Preparing Instructional Objectives.* Palo Alto, Calif.: Fearon Publishers, Inc., 1962.

MILLER, M. W. (ed.). *On Teaching Adults: An Anthology.* Chicago: Center for the Study of Liberal Education for Adults, 1960.

POPHAM, J. W. *The Teacher-empiricist.* Los Angeles: Aegeus Press, 1965.

VALENTINE, C. G. *Programmed Instruction for Electronic Technicians.* Detroit, Mich.: Michigan Bell Telephone Co., 1965.

VENN, G. *Man, Education, and Work: Postsecondary Vocational and Technical Education.* Washington, D. C.: American Council on Education, 1964.

Instructional Media

Audio-Visual Equipment Directory. Fairfax, Va.: National Audio-Visual Assn., published annually.

BROWN, J. W.; LEWIS, R. B.; and HARCLEROAD, F. F. *A-V Instruction: Materials and Methods* (2nd ed.). New York: McGraw-Hill Book Co., Inc., 1964, 592 pages.

DEKIEFFER, R. E. *Audiovisual Instruction.* New York: The Center for Applied Research in Education, 1965, 117 pages.

ERICKSON, C. W. H. *Fundamentals of Teaching with Audiovisual Technology.* New York: The Macmillan Co., 1965, 384 pages.

FARIS, G.; MODLSTAD, J.; and FRYE, H. *Improving the Learning Environment.* (Supt. of Documents Catalog No. FS5.234:34031.) Washington, D. C.: U. S. Government Printing Office, 1964, 148 pages.

Federal Aid for Industrial Arts. Washington, D. C.: American Industrial Arts Assn., National Education Assn., 1201 16th St., N.W., 1966, 92 pages. (Information on instructional aids, equipment, supervision, institutes, research, student assistance, and proposal guidelines.)

KELLEY, C. *A Selective Bibliography on New Media and Vocational Education and Retraining.* (Staff Paper No. 1.) Washington, D.C.: Educational Media Council, 1346 Connecticut Ave., N.W., 1966, 26 pages.

KEMP, J. *Planning and Producing Audiovisual Materials.* San Francisco: Chandler Publishing Co., 1963, 169 pages.

RUFSVOLD, M. I., and GUSS, C. *Guides to Newer Educational Media.* Chicago: American Library Assn., 1961, 74 pages.

SWANSON, E. A. (ed.). *New Media in Teaching the Business Subjects.* Washington, D. C.: National Business Education Assn., National Education Assn., 1201 16th St., N. W., 1965, 206 pages.

WEDBERG, D. P., and BLOODWORTH, M. *Sources of Information on: Educational Media, Organizations, Programs.* Washington, D. C.: Educational Media Council, 1346 Connecticut Ave., N. W., 1967.

WITTICH, W. A., and SCHULLER, C. F. *Audiovisual Materials: Their Nature and Use* (3rd ed.). New York: Harper & Row, Publishers, 1962, 500 pages.

Programmed Instruction

HENDERSHOT, C. H. *Programmed Learning: A Bibliography of Programs and Presentation Devices* (3rd ed.). Bay City, Mich.: Carl H. Hendershot, 1965.

OFIESH, G. D. *Programmed Instruction: A Guide for Management.* New York: American Management Assn., 135 W. 50th St., 1965, 416 pages.

PIPE, P. *Practical Programming.* New York: Holt, Rinehart & Winston, 1966.

TEAL, G. E. (ed.). *Programmed Instruction in Industry and Education.* Stamford, Conn.: Public Research Service, 1963.

Sources of Vocational-technical Instructional Materials

AIAA Publications/Audio-Visual Aids. Washington, D. C.: American Industrial Arts Assn., National Education Assn., 1201 16th St., N.W., revised periodically.

AUBREY, R. H. (ed.). *Selected Free Materials for Classroom Teachers* (rev. ed.). Palo Alto, Calif.: Fearon Publishers, Inc., 1967.

Audio Cardalog. Larchmont, N. Y.: Max U. Bildersee, P. O. Box 989. (Reviews disk recordings and audio tapes; issued monthly, except July and August, on 3″ x 5″ cards.)

Aviation Education Bibliography (4th ed.). Washington, D. C.: National Aerospace Education Council, 1025 Connecticut Ave., N.W., 1964. (A compilation of films, filmstrips, books, periodicals, and other teaching aids related to aviation and flight in the atmosphere.)

Educational Media Index. 14 vols. New York: McGraw-Hill Book Co., Inc., 1964. (A comprehensive listing of all nonprint instructional materials; produced by the Educational Media Council.)

Educators Guide to Free Films. Randolph, Wisc.: Educators Progress Service, revised annually.

Educators Guide to Free Filmstrips. Randolph, Wisc.: Educators Progress Service, revised annually.

Educators Guide to Free Tapes, Scripts, and Transcriptions. Randolph, Wisc.: Educators Progress Service, revised annually.

Film Guide for Industrial Training. Chicago: National Metal Trades Assn., 222 W. Adams St., 1965.

Films on Vocations. New York: Educational Film Library Assn., Inc., 250 W. 57th St., 1955.

Filmstrips and Slide Series of the U. S. Department of Agriculture. (Agriculture Handbook No. 222.) Washington, D. C.: U. S. Government Printing Office, 1963. (Lists materials in the areas of agricultural economics, agricultural engineering, conservation, forestry, 4-H Club activities, historical, home economics, home gardening, livestock, marketing, nutrition, and rural life.)

Free and Inexpensive Materials for Teaching Family Finance. New York: National Committee for Education in Family Finance, 277 Park Ave., 1963. (Annotated list of booklets, films, filmstrips, and other sources in areas of banking, money management, life insurance, investments, Social Security, and taxes.)

Free and Inexpensive Pictures, Pamphlets, and Packets for Air/Space Age Education (6th ed.). Washington, D. C.: National Aerospace Education Council, 1025 Connecticut Ave., N. W., 1966. (Lists approximately 675 items produced by aerospace manufacturers, airlines, government agencies, and private and professional organizations.)

HENDERSHOT, C. H. *Programmed Learning: A Bibliography of Programs and Presentation Devices* (3rd ed.). Bay City, Mich.: Carl H. Hendershot, 1965.

Instructional Materials for Antipoverty and Manpower-training Programs. New York: McGraw-Hill Book Co., Inc., 1965. (Lists films, filmstrips, transparencies, recordings, programmed materials, textbooks, and workbooks published by McGraw-Hill.)

Library of Congress Catalog: Motion Pictures and Filmstrips. Washington, D. C.: Library of Congress, 1953, quarterly with annual and quinquennial cumulations.

Library of Congress Catalog: Music and Phonorecords. Washington, D. C.: Library of Congress, 1953, semi-annual with annual and quinquennial cumulations.

Motion Pictures of the U. S. Department of Agriculture. Washington, D. C.: U. S. Dept. of Agriculture, Office of Information, Motion Picture Service, 1960. Supplement: *Recent Motion Pictures of the U.S.D.A.,* 1963.

National Tape Recording Catalog, 1962-63. Washington, D. C.: Dept. of Audiovisual Instruction, National Education Assn., 1201 16th St., N. W., 1963.

Programmed Instructional Materials, 1964-65. New York. Teachers College Press, Columbia Univ., 1965. (Includes relisting of titles still available contained in *Programs '63.*)

Programs '63: A Guide to Programmed Instructional Materials. Washington, D. C.: U. S. Government Printing Office, 1964. (Produced by the Center for Programmed Instruction.)

Selected Guidance Films and Filmstrips. Washington, D. C.: American Personnel and Guidance Assn., 1605 New Hampshire Ave., N. W., 1966. (Lists materials for use in occupational guidance, counselor education, in-service education, and related settings.)

Selection of Films Available from the U. S. Department of Commerce. Washington, D. C.: Office of Public Information, U. S. Dept. of Commerce, mimeo. (Lists materials available from the Patent Office,

Weather Bureau, Bureau of Standards, Census Bureau, and Bureau of
Public Roads.)

16mm Films for Labor. Washington, D. C.: Dept. of Education, American Federation of Labor and Congress of Industrial Organizations,
815 16th St., N. W., 1964. Supplement, 1965.

Source Directory of 8mm Single Concept Films. Costa Mesa, Calif.:
Technicolor Corp., P. O. Box 517, revised periodically.

U. S. Atomic Energy Commission 16mm Film Catalog, Popular Level.
Washington, D. C.: Div. of Public Information, Audio-Visual Branch,
U. S. Atomic Energy Commission, 1965. (Lists free-loan materials in
17 subject categories for general audiences and elementary, second-
ary, and college students.)

*U. S. Atomic Energy Commission 16mm Motion Picture Film Library,
Professional Level.* Washington, D. C.: Div. of Public Information,
Audio-Visual Branch, U. S. Atomic Energy Commission, 1964. (Lists
free-loan materials of specialized interest to university-level students,
professional scientists, engineers, and technologists.)

U. S. Department of Agriculture Films for Television. Washington, D. C.;
U. S. Government Printing Office, 1963.

U. S. Department of the Interior Bureau of Mines Films, 1965-66.
Washington, D. C.: Office of Information, U. S. Dept. of the Interior,
1966.

U. S. Department of the Interior Film Catalog. Washington, D. C.:
Office of Information, U. S. Dept. of the Interior, 1964. (Lists materials from the Bureau of Reclamation, Bureau of Land Management,
Fish and Wildlife Service, Geological Survey, Bureau of Mines, National Park Service, Alaska Railroad, and Bonneville Power Admin-
istration.)

U. S. Government Films for Public Educational Use — 1963. (Catalog
No. FS5.234:34006-63.) Washington, D. C.: U. S. Government Printing Office, 1964. (Lists films and filmstrips from all agencies of the
executive, judicial, and legislative branches of the federal government; but excludes international organizations, state and local gov-
ernments, and other organizations associated with but not part of
the federal government.)

Visual Aids for Business and Economic Education. Cincinnati, Ohio:
Southwestern Publishing Co., 1965.

Periodicals and Journals

The publications that follow are concerned with educational media,
new techniques, equipment, materials, and research. Articles of particular interest to vocational-technical educators appear constantly.

Audiovisual Instruction. Published monthly except July and August by the Dept. of Audiovisual Instruction, National Education Assn., 1201 16th St., N. W., Washington, D. C. Subscription: $6.00 per year.

AV Communication Review. Published quarterly by the Dept. of Audiovisual Instruction, National Education Assn., 1201 16th St., N. W., Washington, D. C. Subscription: $6.00 per year.

Educational Screen and Audiovisual Guide. Published monthly by Educational Screen, Inc., 434 S. Wabash, Chicago, Ill. Subscription: $4.00 per year.

Educational Technology. Published semimonthly by Educational News Service, P. O. Box 508, Saddle Brook, N. J. 07662. Subscription: $10.00 per year.

NSPI Journal. Published bimonthly by the National Society for Programmed Instruction, Trinity Univ., 715 Stadium Dr., San Antonio, Texas. Subscription: $7.50 per year.

Training in Business and Industry. Published monthly by the Gellert-Wolfman Publishing Corp., 33 W. 60th St., New York, N. Y. Subscription: $5.00 per year.

Also by Robert F. Mager . . .

Quick-reference Checklist from **Analyzing Performance Problems** is available in expanded worksheet form, with space for answers to questions. Professionals will find this worksheet a handy tool, especially in interview situations. In packages of 25 only, $2.00 per package.

Performance Analysis Poster of the flow diagram from *Analyzing Performance Problems* is available as a large (23″ x 35″) 2-color poster.

Measuring Instructional Intent or **Got a Match?** shows how to select or create test items that match the intent of your objectives. The author tells you how to find out whether your instruction is successful. He describes a procedure and offers examples and practice with it that will help you make that critical match between objectives and the test items by which the achievement of those objectives may be measured. Includes an Objective/Item Checklist and Flowchart to use in checking test items.

Goal Analysis explains a procedure that will help you describe the meaning of the goals you hope to achieve—whether these goals deal with attitudes, appreciations, or understandings—so that you will be able to make better decisions toward their achievement and recognize progress and success. The goal analysis procedure is often critical in the development of meaningful and *achievable* objectives.

Analyzing Performance Problems or **'You Really Oughta Wanna'** (with Peter Pipe) is a practical approach to problems of human performance—when someone isn't doing what someone else expects him to do. The authors explain a procedure for analyzing such problems, and point the reader in the direction of solutions that will work. Anyone who directs or guides the performance of others will find this book extremely helpful.

Developing Attitude Toward Learning shows teachers how to recognize student behaviors that can be used as evidence of favorable (or unfavorable) attitude toward the subjects they are teaching. Dr. Mager describes three principles teachers can apply to help their students have more favorable attitude toward their subjects, and offers a way of measuring success and a technique for improving upon it.

Preparing Instructional Objectives is a cornerstone book in the current reshaping of American education (and it has also been published in 12 foreign-language editions). In it, Dr. Mager effectively demonstrates how to *define* teaching objectives, how to *state* them clearly, and how to describe criteria by which to measure success. Any person developing materials for instructional use will want to keep this book close at hand.

 Lear Siegler, Inc. / Fearon Publishers
6 Davis Drive, Belmont, California 94002